SEX AND SANITY

CHRISTIAN FOUNDATIONS

A series edited by

PHILIP E. HUGHES

Sex and Sanity

A CHRISTIAN VIEW OF SEXUAL MORALITY

by

STUART BARTON BABBAGE

THE WESTMINSTER PRESS
Philadelphia

Published by The Westminster Press ®
Philadelphia, Pennsylvania

PRINTED IN THE UNITED STATES OF AMERICA

CONTENTS

FOREWORD

IF in the Victorian era sex was a subject not to be mentioned, in our day it has become something that is spoken and written about with few (in some cases no) inhibitions and indeed almost compulsively. This applies not merely to what has hitherto been regarded as normal sexual behavior but also, and at least equally, to sex in its abnormal and perverted expressions—so much so that we are now well on the way to becoming a generation obsessed with sex. The old decencies and restraints are despised. Privacy is largely a thing of the past. Promiscuity is praised by voices both inside and outside the church. Perverted practices are condoned as an acceptable "morality" for those who indulge in them—or if they are deplored, it is as a symptom of sickness, not of sin. The Christian, at least, should be constant in proclaiming the possibility and reality of victory through Christ over sexual as well as all other kinds of temptation to do what is contrary to the will of God.

The Surgeon General, according to press reports, has said that in the U.S.A., 1,500 persons contract a venereal disease every day in the year. Syphilis has increased by 200 percent from 1965 to 1966, among persons under twenty. The rate of illegitimate pregnancies among teenagers doubled from 1940 to 1961, and it quadrupled among women in the age level twenty to twenty-five. . . . Fifty percent of teen-age girls who marry are pregnant; 80 percent of those marry teen-age boys. It is estimated that nearly 200,000 teen-agers resort to abortion every year.

Alarm over a situation that shows every sign of rapid deterioration was expressed by no less august, and religiously neutral, a body than the British Medical Association in a report on Venereal Disease and Young People, published in 1964. The statistics speak for themselves. Between the years 1957 and 1961 there was a population increase in the fifteen to twenty-four age group of 10 percent in Great Britain, but the increase in cases of gonorrhea treated for this same age group over this period was 67 percent. Illegitimate maternities increased by some 300 percent. It is important to notice also that, according to the report, homosexual activity, which has become widespread, so far from being clinically innocuous, has contributed materially to the spreading of venereal disease. The vital importance of chastity, both for the individual and for society as a whole, is emphatically stated, for not only is the exercise of self-control in itself "a valuable preparation for marriage" (contrary to much cheap theorizing that is heard nowadays), but also "the maintenance of the Christian ideal of chastity is of the utmost importance not only in combating the sexually contracted diseases but also in preserving the institution of marriage and the family unit, on which our way of life is founded." The admonition is given that "anything which debases this is a threat to our society." This counsel, coming from such a source, should be seriously heeded by both young and old.

In the pages that follow, Dr. Babbage examines searchingly the situation in which we find ourselves at the present time and enunciates afresh the Christian understanding of sexual morality.

P. E. H.

ACKNOWLEDGMENTS

The author would like to thank the following for giving him their permission to quote:

David Mace and The National Marriage Guidance Council, for quotations from his booklet *The Outlook for Marriage.*

British Medical Journal, for a quotation from their booklet *V. D. and Young People.*

Her Majesty's Stationery Office, for short extracts from Command Paper *Cmnd 247, Report of the Committee on Homosexual Offences and Prostitution.*

The Church of England Committee for Diocesan Moral and Social Welfare Councils, for quotations from their booklet *Sexual Offenders and Social Punishment.*

Longmans, Green & Co., Ltd., for a quotation from *The Vision of God,* by K. E. Kirk.

Cambridge University Press, for quotations from *Soundings,* edited by A. R. Vidler.

Constable & Co., Ltd., for a quotation from *A Genuinely Human Existence,* by Stephen Neill.

SCM Press, Ltd., for a quotation from *Christian Morals Today,* by John A. T. Robinson.

CHAPTER ONE

THE BODY

"Fearfully and wonderfully made"
—Ps. 139:14

MAN has always been a subject of perplexity to himself. In the familiar words of Alexander Pope:

> *He hangs between; in doubt to act or rest;*
> *In doubt to deem himself a god, or beast;*
> *In doubt his mind or body to prefer;*
> *Born but to die, and reas'ning but to err;*
> *Alike in ignorance, his reason such,*
> *Whether he thinks too little or too much;*
> *Chaos of thought and passion, all confused;*
> *Still by himself abused, or disabused;*
> *Created half to rise, and half to fall;*
> *Great lord of all things, yet a prey to all;*
> *Sole judge of truth, in endless error hurled;*
> *The glory, jest, and riddle of the world!*[1]

This is man's predicament: is he "to deem himself a god, or beast"? Is his body an evil encumbrance, a source of cloying contamination, or is it altogether glorious? Is sex inherently disgusting or is it wholly good? Or is sex a matter neither for embarrassed apology nor for un-inhibited enjoyment but for reverent and responsible use according to the will of God?

C. S. Lewis says that, broadly speaking, there are three different views of the body. He summarizes them as fol-

[1] *Essay on Man*, Ep. ii, 1.7–18.

11

lows: "First there is that of those ascetic Pagans who called it the prison or the 'tomb' of the soul, and of Christians like Fisher to whom it was a 'sack of dung,' food for worms, filthy, shameful, a source of nothing but temptation to bad men and humiliation of good ones. Then there are the Neo-Pagans . . . the nudists and the sufferers from Dark Gods, to whom the body is glorious. But thirdly we have the view which St. Francis expressed by calling his body 'Brother Ass.'" Historically, he suggests, man has tended to oscillate uneasily between contemptuous denigration and extravagant exaltation, whereas what is required, he implies, is glad and grateful acceptance. Enlarging on the metaphor of Francis of Assisi, C. S. Lewis writes: "Ass is exquisitely right because no-one in his senses can either revere or hate a donkey. It is a useful, sturdy, lazy, obstinate, patient, lovable and infuriating beast; deserving now the stick and now the carrot; both pathetically and absurdly beautiful. So the body."[2]

It will be a profitable exercise to examine, in a little more detail, these different views.

DUALISTIC VIEWS

The Pythagoreans, in a familiar jingle, affirmed that the body is a tomb (*soma-sema*). According to Philolaus the body is a house of detention in which the soul is imprisoned to expiate its sin.[3] Epictetus referred to himself as "a poor soul shackled to a corpse."[4] Seneca spoke contemptuously of "the detestable habitation" of the body.[5] Marcus Aurelius urged his contemporaries to "disdain"

[2] *The Four Loves* (Harcourt, Brace & World, Inc., 1960), pp. 116–117.

[3] Quoted by William Barclay in *Flesh and Spirit* (Abingdon Press, 1962), p. 10.

[4] *Fragment* 23.

[5] *Letters* 92.110.

the body which is, he said, only "blood and bones and network, a twisted skein of nerves, veins, arteries."[6]

This point of view finds classic expression in Plato's account of Socrates' last hours: "For the body is a source of endless trouble to us by reason of the mere requirement of food; and is liable also to diseases which overtake and impede us in the search after true being: it fills us full of loves, and lusts, and fears, and fancies of all kinds, and endless foolery, and in fact, as men say, takes away from us the power of thinking at all. Whence come wars, and fightings, and factions? Whence but from the body and the lusts of the body? . . . It has been proved to us by experience that if we would have pure knowledge of anything we must be quit of the body—the soul in herself must behold things in themselves: and then we shall attain the wisdom which we desire, and of which we say that we are lovers; not while we live, but after death; for if while in company with the body, the soul cannot have pure knowledge, one of two things follows—either knowledge is not to be attained at all, or, if at all, after death. For then, and not till then, the soul will be parted from the body and exist in herself alone. In this present life, I reckon that we make the nearest approach to knowledge when we have the least possible intercourse or communion with the body, and are not surfeited with the bodily nature, but keep ourselves pure until the hour when God Himself is pleased to release us. And thus having got rid of the foolishness of the body we shall be pure and hold converse with the pure, and know of ourselves the clear light everywhere which is no other than the light of truth."[7]

The Hellenized Jew Philo, who was the contemporary of Paul, echoing Plato, described the body as a prison and

6 *Meditations* 2.2.
7 *Phaedo* 65c–66a.

13

a corpse.[8] "It is not easy," he laments, "to believe in God because of the mortal companion (that is, the flesh) with which we are yoked."[9]

For the Gnostics the body was more than a matter of unhappy regret; it was a source of contamination and an invitation to sin. Marcion urged his followers to escape the corruption and degradation of the body either by embracing celibacy or by practicing continence within marriage.[10] Some Gnostics did not hesitate to say that marriage is "a foul and polluted way of life" and that entrance into eternal life is impossible for those who continue therein. In the apocryphal Acts of John coitus is described as "an experiment of the serpent . . . the impediment which separates from the Lord, the beginning of disobedience, the end of life, and death."[11] Tertullian informed his wife that between marriage and fornication there is merely a legal and not an intrinsic difference, since "the shameful act which constitutes its essence is the same as fornication."[12]

Sherwin Bailey, in an exhaustive discussion of *The Sexual Relation in Christian Thought,* notes "the embarrassment, suspicion, antipathy, and abhorrence variously displayed by many of the Fathers towards physical sexuality,"[13] culminating in Augustine's virtual identification of coitus with sin.

This morbid fear of sex explains why it was that so many of the church fathers sought to suppress all natural affection. "Should your little nephew hang on your neck,"

[8] *De Migratione* 2; *De Agricultura* 5.
[9] *Q.R.D.H.* 18.
[10] Quoted by Roland H. Bainton in *Sex, Love and Marriage* (see page 5) (Fontana, William Collins Sons & Co., Ltd., 1958), p. 27.
[11] Quoted by D. S. Bailey in *Sexual Relation in Christian Thought* (Harper & Brothers, 1959), p. 40.
[12] *De Exhortatione Castitatis.*
[13] (Harper & Brothers, 1959), p. 98.

Jerome writes, "pay no heed. Should your mother, with ashes on her hair and garments rent, display the breasts at which she nursed you, be adamant. Should your father prostrate himself on the threshold, trample him under your foot and go your way. With dry eyes fly to the standard of the cross. In such cases cruelty is the only true affection."[14]

"Throughout the vast literature of Monasticism," Herbert Workman notes, "there runs one constant refrain, the apostrophe of the dying Pachomius to his body: 'Alas, why was I ever attached to thee, and why should I suffer because of thee an eternal condemnation!' "[15] There were some monks who regarded it as a snare, if not a sin, to bathe, because of the danger of seeing themselves undressed. Athanasius boasted that Anthony "never changed his vest nor washed his feet," and his example was held up for pious emulation.[16] Cleanliness of the body, it was held, was the pollution of the soul. Antonius proudly related that such was the holy asceticism of Simeon Stylites that when he walked, vermin dropped from his body. "The church killed the bath," Havelock Ellis accuses.[17]

In their fierce determination to subdue the body and to escape the enticements of the flesh, these ascetics systematically neglected hygiene and health. What W. E. H. Lecky bluntly calls this "hideous maceration of the body"[18] found its horrifying culmination in Origen's barbaric act of self-emasculation.

---

14 *Post-Nicene Fathers*, VI, 14.
15 *The Evolution of the Monastic Ideal* (Beacon Press, Inc., 1962), p. 63.
16 Quoted in Workman, *op. cit.*, p. 64.
17 *Ibid.*
18 *History of European Morals from Augustus to Charlemagne* (George Braziller, Inc., 1955), II, p. 107.

Today, we are experiencing a reaction of excess. What is required, D. H. Lawrence says, is not an attitude of timid rejection but of joyous acceptance. "I always labour at the same thing," he insists, "to make the sex relation valid and precious instead of shameful."[19] "Give me the body," he cries. "I believe the life of the body is a greater reality than the life of the mind; when the body is really awakened to life. . . . The human body is only just coming to real life. With the Greeks it gave a lovely flicker, then Plato and Aristotle killed it, and Jesus finished it off. But now the body is coming really to life."[20]

Lawrence's philosophy finds characteristic expression in his novel *Lady Chatterley's Lover*. The publication of a paperback edition, in unexpurgated form, precipitated a celebrated prosecution under the Obscene Publications Act (*Regina v. Penguin Books Limited*). In the subsequent trial the Bishop of Woolwich (John A. T. Robinson) appeared as a witness for the defense. He explained that Lawrence was trying to portray sexual relations "as in a real sense something sacred, as in a real sense an act of holy communion." For Lawrence, he explained, "flesh was completely sacramental of spirit." "His description of sexual relations," he continued, "cannot be taken out of the context of his . . . astonishing sensitivity to the beauty and value of all organic relationships." "Some of his descriptions of nature in the book seem to me," he said, "to be extraordinarily beautiful and delicate."[21] At this

[19] Quoted by Elizabeth Hamill in *These Modern Writers* (Melbourne: Georgian House Pty., Ltd., 1946), p. 95.

[20] *Lady Chatterley's Lover* (London: The Vanguard Library, William Heinemann Ltd., 1953), p. 187.

[21] C. H. Rolph, ed., *The Trial of Lady Chatterley* (Harmondsworth, Middlesex: Penguin Books Ltd., 1961), pp. 70–71.

point Mr. Justice Byrne interposed. "Does it," he asked, "portray the life of an immoral woman?" The bishop gave a qualified reply: "It portrays the life of a woman in an immoral relationship, insofar as adultery is an immoral relationship."[22]

Canon J. N. D. Kelly points out that untrammeled naturalism makes of sex an absolute.[23] Lawrence recognized this. "I realize that marriage, or something like it," he admitted, "is essential, and that the old Church knew best the enduring needs of man, beyond the spasmodic needs of today and yesterday." Then he added, characteristically: "But—and this 'but' crashes through our hearts like a bullet—marriage is no marriage that is not basically and permanently phallic, and that is not linked up with the sun and the earth, the moon and the fixed stars and the planets, in the rhythm of days, in the rhythm of months, in the rhythm of quarters, of years, of decades, of centuries."[24]

Idolatry, the apostle Paul charges (Rom. 1:22 f.), is indissolubly linked with immorality, so that they that make idols become like them (Ps. 106:36 ff.). To make an idol of sex is to degrade love into lust and sex into sensuality.

Charles Raven asks the pertinent question: "Is there really any true lover, any happily married pair, any family, which believes in the Lawrence doctrine that a perfect copulation is the sole, or indeed the primary, element in sexual union? or doubts that to talk about it

---

22 *Ibid.*, p. 72. We shall discuss in the penultimate chapter the validity of "the new morality"; at this point it is sufficient to note the bishop's claim that "nothing can of itself always be labelled 'wrong.'"

23 Sermon preached in the University Church of St. Mary the Virgin, Oxford, 1964, as reported in the *Church of England Newspaper*.

24 Quoted in Rolph, *op. cit.*, pp. 161–162.

in four-letter words is to degrade it by setting it apart from the infinite joys and sanctities of marriage?" Marriage, he continues, is "a sharing of work and play, of thought and prayer, of suffering and ecstasy," in which, of course, "the sex act has a special and representative and culminating place."[25]

THE BIBLICAL VIEW

The Bible lends no support either to the defamation of the body or to its deification. "The body," Paul affirms, "is not for fornication, but for the Lord." (I Cor. 6:13.) "I beseech you therefore, brethren," the apostle writes, "by the mercies of God, that ye present your bodies a living sacrifice, holy, acceptable unto God." (Rom. 12:1.) The body, the Bible teaches, is to be disciplined and dedicated to the service of God: it is to be rightly used and not abused (I Cor. 7:31).

"Everything created by God is good," the apostle insists, "and nothing is to be rejected if it is received with thanksgiving; for then it is consecrated by the word of God and prayer." (I Tim. 4:4-5, RSV.) The body, as part of God's creation, is "good" and not "nasty"; it is to be "received" and not "rejected"; it is to be held in honor and treated with respect. The body is emphatically not evil, although it can, unhappily, be prostituted in the service of evil and made the instrument of sin. Luther, in his illuminating way, points out that our Lord, who was sinless, had a body, and that the devil, who is sinful, is without a body.[26] The body is not, as Plato taught, a tomb; rather, it is, in the words of the apostle Paul, a

[25] "Sex and Sacrament," *Frontier* (Spring, 1961), Vol. 4, p. 19.
[26] Quoted by Oscar E. Feucht in *Sex and the Church*, Marriage and Family Research Series, Vol. 5 (Concordia Publishing House, 1961), p. 77.

temple of the Holy Ghost (I Cor. 6:19). It is not, in the language of dualism, dirty and disgusting; on the contrary, it is a thing of excellent beauty. It is, in the memorable words of the psalmist, "fearfully and wonderfully made" (Ps. 139:14).

The body is an essential part of man's constitution. After forming man "of the dust of the ground," God "breathed into his nostrils the breath of life; and man became a living soul" (Gen. 2:7). Thus, we ought to think of man not as an incarnated soul but rather (to appropriate Wheeler Robinson's helpful phrase) as an animated body.[27] Man's body is not an encumbrance and a hindrance; on the contrary, it is a necessary part of man's essential being.

This explains why it is that the distinctive Christian doctrine of the life to come is not a doctrine of immortality but of resurrection. Christians do not look forward to a state of disembodied existence; they look forward to a fuller and richer life in which the body is a perfect instrument of the spirit. This present body is but "a tent," ready to be pulled down; it will be replaced by something far more permanent, "a house," eternal in the heavens. This body is subject to sin and sickness; that body which is to be will be resplendent and altogether glorious (I Cor. 15:35 f.). "In this we groan," the apostle writes, "earnestly desiring to be clothed upon with our house which is from heaven: if so be that being clothed we shall not be found naked. For we that are in this tabernacle do groan, being burdened: not for that we would be unclothed, but clothed upon, that mortality might be swallowed up of life." (II Cor. 5:2–4.)

27 *The Christian Doctrine of Man* (Edinburgh: T. & T. Clark, 1911), p. 27.

CHAPTER TWO

SEXUALITY

"Male and female created he them"

—Gen. 1:27

PLATO affirms that in all men there is a sense of longing, an awareness of incompleteness, a hunger for wholeness. In the *Symposium*, through the mouth of Aristophanes, Plato expresses the view that human beings were originally spherical or globular in shape and that they were punished for their pride in trying to carry heaven by assault by being cut in two. "It is from this distant epoch that we may date the innate love which human beings feel for one another, the love which restores us to our ancient state by attempting to weld together two beings into one and to heal the wounds which humanity suffered." "Each of us," he continues, "is the mere broken tally of a man, the result of a bisection which has reduced us to a condition like that of flat fish, and each of us is perpetually in search of his corresponding tally."[1]

In all men, Plato says, there is a "longing," a longing that cannot be expressed but only obscurely hinted at. Lucretius expresses the same thought. "When a man is pierced by the shafts of Venus," the Latin philosopher writes, "he strives towards the source of the wound and craves to be united with it." "His speechless yearning is a presentiment of bliss." "This is what we term Venus.

[1] Translated by W. Hamilton (Harmondsworth, Middlesex: Penguin Books, Ltd., 1951), p. 62.

This is the origin of the thing called love—that drop of Venus' honey that first drips into our heart, to be followed by numbing heart-ache."[2]

Man is restlessly aware that, for the full enjoyment of life, and the satisfaction of life's necessities, he needs the companionship of another. Many colloquial phrases express this conviction. A man will speak of his "other half"; at other times he will speak, in jocular vein, of his "better half."

The Bible, however, lends no support to the mythical view that human beings were originally androgynous. Man, according to the Bible, exists in a state of sexual polarity, of complementary differentiation, by the ordinance of God, by the fact that "male and female created he them" (Gen. 1:27).

THE DIFFERENTIATION OF THE SEXES

Man's creation marked the climax and culmination of God's creative activity. God, having finished his work of creation, pronounced it "very good" (Gen. 1:31); concerning the fact that man was alone, however, he said: "It is not good" (ch. 2:18). God gave Adam lordship over the created world: "over the fish of the sea, and over the fowl of the air, and over the cattle, and over all the earth, and over every creeping thing that creepeth upon the earth" (ch. 1:26). Adam was given lordship, but he still lacked companionship: "for Adam there was not found a help meet for him" (ch. 2:20). God met Adam's need: "And the Lord God caused a deep sleep to fall upon Adam, and he slept: and he took one of his ribs, and closed up the flesh instead thereof; and the rib, which the Lord God had taken from man, made he a woman, and

2 *The Nature of the Universe,* translated by R. E. Latham (Harmondsworth, Middlesex: Penguin Books, Ltd., 1951), p. 163.

21

brought her unto the man. And Adam said, This is now bone of my bones, and flesh of my flesh: she shall be called Woman, because she was taken out of Man." (Vs. 21–23.)

The church fathers found a wealth of suggestive symbolism in the picturesque details. Woman was not taken, Peter Lombard ingeniously points out, from the head of man, for she was not intended to be his ruler, nor from his foot, for she was not intended to be his slave, but from his side, for she was to be his companion and his comfort. Man, according to the rabbis, is restless while he misses the rib that was taken out of his side, and woman is restless till she gets under man's arm, from whence she was taken.[3] God, Tertullian comments, "first subtracted woman from man, and then, in the mathematics of marriage, added two together again who had originally been substantially one."[4]

"So God created man . . . male and female created he them." (Gen. 1:27.) Man, by the will of God, exists in a twofold state of sexual differentiation and polarity. Karl Barth makes the fine comment: "God His Creator requires that he should be genuinely and fully the one or the other, male or female, that he should acknowledge his sex instead of trying in some way to deny it, that he should rejoice in it rather than be ashamed of it, that he should fruitfully use its potentialities rather than neglect them, that he should stick to its limits rather than seek in some way to transcend them."[5] Concerning the sexes,

[3] Quoted by David R. Mace in *Whom God Hath Joined* (The Westminster Press, 1953), p. 60.

[4] "To His Wife," *Treatises on Marriage and Remarriage,* Ancient Christian Writers, Vol. 13 (London: Longmans, Green & Co., Ltd., 1951), p. 12.

[5] *The Doctrine of Creation,* Vol. III of *Church Dogmatics,* ed. by G. W. Bromiley and T. F. Torrance (Edinburgh: T. & T. Clark, 1961), Pt. 4, p. 149.

Barth says: "In every situation, in face of every task and in every conversation, their functions and possibilities, when they are obedient to the command, will be distinctive and diverse, and will never be interchangeable. . . . A desire which . . . might include jealousy, envy, intimidation or usurpation can never in any circumstances be good, whereas a pure desire will constantly and surely lead a man and a woman back to their place."[6]

Nothing but confusion will result from the attempt to disrupt and disturb the given distinctions between the sexes. A woman's glory is her femininity; a man's glory is his masculinity: the differences between the sexes are to be affirmed and not denied. The Bible, for example, unequivocally condemns such sexual aberrations as transvestism (Deut. 22:5).

The Bible not only recognizes the fact that there are two sexes; it also recognizes that the two sexes belong to each other and are directed toward each other. There is a mutual relationship of belonging. This relationship finds its fitting expression and perfect consummation in the act of physical intercourse. "Coitus without coexistence," Barth insists, "is demonic";[7] but, as the symbol and seal of coexistence, it is love's proper prerogative and precious privilege.

The Biblical attitude toward sex is positive and accepting. Sex, the Bible teaches, is one of God's good gifts, and it has been given us richly to enjoy (I Tim. 6:17). To the classical Greeks sex was, at the best, a necessary evil, and, at the worst, a slavery to the lowest passions. The God of the Bible, however, is a God who commands his children to "be fruitful, and multiply, and replenish the earth" (Gen. 1:28); a God who says that a man is "to take a wife for himself in holiness and honor" (I Thess. 4:4, RSV).

6 *Ibid.*, p. 154.
7 *Ibid.*, p. 133.

The Bible lends no support to those who would exalt celibacy to the derogation and neglect of matrimony. "Forbidding to marry" is expressly designated as one of "the doctrines of devils" (I Tim. 4:1,3). According to the book of Proverbs, one of the three or four things too wonderful for human understanding is, significantly enough, "the way of a man with a maid" (Prov. 30:19).

Jesus, in answer to a trick question by the Sadducees about the resurrection, replied that "in the resurrection they neither marry, nor are given in marriage" (Matt. 22:30). If this is so, would it not be better, some argued, for a man not to touch a woman? (I Cor. 7:1.) If marriage belongs to this life alone, why not anticipate the blessedness of the age to come? Why not abstain here and now? Paul points out, by way of reply, that each man has his gift from God: God calls some to marriage and some to celibacy. God calls some to celibacy to enable them to give themselves without distraction to the work of the Lord (vs. 32 f.). J. J. von Allmen, commenting on Paul's words, says: "Celibacy cannot be justified by the desire to be alone, by egoism and scorn of the opposite sex, nor above all on the basis of a metaphysical dualism which would see in the insistence and demands of the body so many obstacles to purity of Christian life and walking in Christ. It is justified only when liberating him who assumes it to be totally at the disposal of and in the service of the Lord."[8] As celibacy cannot be justified, except it be "in the Lord," so marriage, too, must be "in the Lord" (v. 39). Marriage is still, in this life, Paul points out, a proper and legitimate form of Christian vocation.

Nevertheless, Paul recognizes that because of what he calls "the present distress" (I Cor. 7:26) and the imminent

[8] *Pauline Teaching on Marriage* (London: Faith Press, Ltd., 1963), p. 16.

24

end of the age (v. 29), there is a case for abstinence. He does not suggest that marriage is evil or that sex is unclean: it is the fact that Christ is coming again. His argument is apocalyptic and not dualistic. Marriage, he emphatically insists, is an honorable estate. "Have I no right," he asks, "to take a Christian wife about with me, like the rest of the apostles and the Lord's brothers, and Cephas?" (Ch. 9:5, NEB.) He personally wishes that some would elect to remain single (this, he adds, he says by way of permission and not by commandment). Nevertheless, it is right for most men to marry to avoid temptation (ch. 7:2).

Paul says that he has no commandment of the Lord concerning celibacy (I Cor. 7:25). He freely admits that there are advantages in relation to the work of the ministry in being unencumbered (v. 34); but he also recognizes that there are problems arising from man's sensual nature which cannot be ignored (v. 9). There are advantages in being single, "but," he repeats, "if thou marry, thou hast not sinned; and if a virgin marry, she hath not sinned" (v. 28). The important thing is that a man should not be tempted and tormented by sensual desire and that he should be "free from anxious care" (v. 32, NEB).

THE CONSEQUENCE OF THE FALL

The consequence of the Fall, in relation to sex, has been disruption and disorder. Those who, by God's appointment, were intended to live together in fellowship and mutual love, have ceased to be partners and become rivals. God, in pronouncing judgment on Eve, said: "Thy desire shall be to thy husband, and he shall rule over thee" (Gen. 3:16). Here, Helmut Thielicke says, we have not so much a commandment as a prognostic curse. "Now it is promised that the sexes will be 'against' each other and the question is who shall triumph and who shall be subjugated. Now libido-thralldom on the one hand and despotism on the other constitute a terrible correspondency."[9] This antagonism becomes apparent, he notes, in the fact that Adam and Eve immediately proceed to denounce one another (v. 12).

As a consequence of the Fall, Adam and Eve were immediately conscious of a sense of guilty shame. Prior to the Fall, "they were both naked, the man and his wife, and were not ashamed" (Gen. 2:25). They were as God had created them, without self-consciousness or shame; they had no cause for envy or rivalry because they had nothing to hide or conceal. As a consequence of the Fall, however, "the eyes of them both were opened, and they knew that they were naked; and they sewed fig leaves together, and made themselves aprons" (ch. 3:7). They became aware of their own sexuality. Not only did they self-consciously seek to hide the evidence of their own sexuality by sewing fig leaves together, they also guiltily sought to hide themselves from the presence of the Lord among the trees of the garden.

Sex, in the life of fallen man, is no longer an unalloyed good, but a matter of perplexity and embarrassment. Man's control over the activity of his sexual organs is, Augustine argues, only partial and incomplete. Adam's disobedience, Augustine observes, in one of his anti-Pelagian tractates, "was followed by the penalty of man's finding his own members emulating against himself that very disobedience which he had practised against God. Then, abashed at their action, since they moved no more at the bidding of his rational will, but at their own arbitrary choice, as it were, instigated by lust, he devised the covering which should conceal such of them as he

[9] *The Ethics of Sex* (Harper & Row, Publishers, Inc., 1964), p. 8.

26

judged to be worthy of shame." Because of the disobedience of our members and the fact of shame, Augustine writes, an element has come into human sexuality
since the Fall that is both a consequence and a cause of
sin. This element is concupiscence or lust. Consequently,
he insists, an element of lust is inseparable from fallen
sexuality, even in Christian marriage.[10]

For man, in his fallen state, sex tends to be a matter
of compulsive preoccupation and anxious concern. C. S.
Lewis, in his vivid epigrammatic way, writes: "You can
get a large audience together for a strip-tease act—that is,
to watch a girl undress on the stage: now suppose you
came to a country where you could fill a theatre by simply
bringing a covered plate on the stage and then slowly
lifting the cover so as to let every one see, just before the
lights went out, that it contained a mutton chop or a bit
of bacon, wouldn't you think that in that country something had gone wrong with the appetite for food? And
wouldn't anyone who had grown up in a different world
think there was something equally queer about the state
of the sex instinct among us?"[11]

C. S. Lewis notes a further fact: that men find perennial pleasure in coarse jokes. (This provides additional
support, he believes, for the view that man is a "fallen"
being. The Fall explains why it is that man's present life
is characterized by confusion and contradiction.) "The
coarse joke proclaims that we have here an animal which
finds its own animality either objectionable or funny.
Unless there had been a quarrel between the spirit and
the organism I do not see how this could be: it is the very

10 *De Matrimonio et Concupiscentia*. Quoted by John Langdon-
Davies in *Sex, Sin and Sanctity* (London: Victor Gollancz, 1954),
pp. 97 f.
11 *Christian Behaviour* (London: Geoffrey Bles, 1943), p. 27.

mark of the two not being 'at home' together. But it is very difficult to imagine such a state of affairs as original —to suppose a creature which from the very first was half shocked and half tickled to death at the mere fact of being the creature it is. I do not perceive that dogs see anything funny about being dogs: I suspect that angels see nothing funny about being angels."[12]

The ordinary man finds sex perplexing, explosive, and destructive. As a consequence of the Fall, what was meant for man's blessing has become a burden and what was bestowed as a privilege has become a problem. Christians believe that, to handle sex aright, we need the forgiving and enabling grace of God.

SEXUAL KNOWLEDGE

"The mystery of sex," Thielicke rightly stresses, "cannot possibly be explained by any objectifying method—the scientific method, for example. That mystery is unveiled in the temple of love, but not in the laboratory. Sexual knowledge is qualitatively different from knowledge about sex."[13]

The Bible describes the act of coitus as a kind of knowing. "Adam knew Eve his wife; and she conceived, and bare Cain." (Gen. 4:1.) In the sexual experience a man comes to "know" his wife; he learns, for the first time, something about his wife that he did not know before and that he could learn in no other way. He learns to "know" her in the deep intimacy of her being.

The mystery of sexuality is something different from physiological knowledge. The deep mystery of the sexual experience can never be explained: it can only be experienced. It can never be discovered from without, but only

12 *Miracles* (The Macmillan Company, 1947), p. 154.
13 *Op. cit.*, p. 66.

from within. It is in and through the experience of intercourse that the mystery is unveiled.

"Part of the importance of sexual intercourse," Sherwin Bailey points out, "is that it affords husband and wife a medium for those mutual disclosures for which no words can be found; the senses become the channel of communication for all that lies too deep for utterance and yet must somehow be told."[14]

In the act of intercourse a man and a woman become, in Biblical language, "one flesh": they enter into a relationship that is as private as it is personal. The physical relationship seals and symbolizes an underlying unity of heart and mind. For the man, it is associated with a joyous sense of exhilarating achievement; for the woman, with an equally joyous sense of ecstatic abandon: for both, it is, what Barth calls, "a blessed frenzy, a breathtaking dialectic of self-fulfillment and self-forgetfulness."[15] It is the sublime fulfillment, and the sacred ratification of love.

[14] *The Mystery of Love and Marriage* (Harper & Row, Publishers, Inc., 1952), p. 60.
[15] *Op. cit.*, p. 120.

CHAPTER THREE

LOVE

"A most vehement flame"
—S. of Sol. 8:6

LOVE, in the Bible, means not only ecstatic joy but willing duty, not only love as a consuming passion, "a most vehement flame," but love as a deep dedication, "for better or worse, for richer or poorer, in sickness and in health."

In our Western society, it is usual to interpret love in terms of emotion and desire. In the Bible, however, love is not so much a passion as a persuasion; not so much a matter of the glands as a matter of the will. Love, in the Bible, means to obey and to serve; it does not mean to be giddy and sentimental. "In contradistinction to mere affection," Karl Barth points out, "love may be recognized by the fact that it is determined, and indeed determined upon the life-partnership of marriage. Love does not question; it gives an answer. Love does not think; it knows. Love does not hesitate; it acts. Love does not fall into raptures; it is ready to undertake responsibilities."[1] Love is a settled disposition of the will; it is not forever coming and going. Thus Abraham's love for Sarah was quiet and steadfast, and Jacob, out of love for Rachel, was willing to endure fourteen years of protracted servitude, "and they seemed unto him but a few days, for the love he had to her" (Gen. 29:20).

[1] *Op. cit.*, p. 221.

The Bible recognizes that respect is love's prerequisite. A man, according to the commandment, is to "honor" his father and his mother. Respect, the Bible teaches, is the necessary precondition of love.[2] (Interestingly enough, sociologists suggest that it is precisely because children today no longer respect their parents that they turn to crime. In recent years nearly half of all the indictable offenses in England have been committed by young people under the age of twenty-one. "No doubt the causes of delinquency are extremely complex," C. H. and Winifred M. Whiteley write in *The Permissive Morality*, "but the principal cause of this recent expansion of juvenile crime is . . . the emancipation of young people from effective adult control."[3] Parents who abdicate their responsibilities forfeit respect, and in forfeiting respect, they forfeit love.)

Not only is a man to "honor" his father and his mother; according to the commandment, he is to "love" God. "Thou shalt love the Lord thy God with all thine heart, and with all thy soul, and with all thy might." (Deut. 6:5.) A man might protest that the affections cannot be commanded, and that the one thing that cannot be commanded is love. But love, in the Bible, is an affair of the will rather than of the heart, and what is commanded is respect, not emotion.[4] Thus the beginning of wisdom is the "fear" of the Lord (Prov. 9:10).

2 See William Graham Cole, *Sex and Love in the Bible* (Association Press, 1959).

3 (London: Methuen & Co., Ltd., 1964), p. 33.

4 "Only if love is thought of as an emotion is it meaningless to command love; the *command* of love shows that love is understood as an attitude of the will." Rudolf Bultmann, *Jesus and the Word* (Charles Scribner's Sons, 1958), p. 118.

Respect is indispensable. No man can love one whom he despises. A man may patronize, a man may pity, but, if respect is absent, he cannot love. That is why, within marriage, respect is fundamental. Respect excludes exploitation; it makes possible mutual consideration and concern.

LOVE AS DESIRE

Within the context of marriage, duty is progressively supplanted by delight and obligation by joy. Love, in its glorious fruition, becomes (to quote the Song of Solomon) "a most vehement flame," as passionate and "hungry as the sea."

In the Song of Solomon we have a series of magnificent lyrics in praise of love. Concerning love, the conclusion is: "Its flashes are flashes of fire" (S. of Sol. 8:6, RSV).

With a wealth of concrete imagery the swain sings the beauty of the beloved. "Your eyes," he cries, "are doves behind your veil." (S. of Sol. 4:1, RSV.) "Your lips," he repeats, "are like a scarlet thread, and your mouth is lovely." (V. 3, RSV.) "You are all fair, my love; there is no flaw in you." (V. 7, RSV.) He confesses: "You have ravished my heart, my sister, my bride, you have ravished my heart with a glance of your eyes" (v. 9, RSV). She is equally uninhibited: "My beloved is all radiant and ruddy, distinguished among ten thousand" (ch. 5:10, RSV). She joyfully exclaims: "I am my beloved's, and his desire is toward me" (ch. 7:10, RSV). She testifies: "I am my beloved's, and my beloved is mine" (ch. 6:3, RSV). She freely confesses: "I am sick with love" (ch. 5:8, RSV).

The poem ends with the triumphant declaration that "love is strong as death" (S. of Sol. 8:6, RSV). It is unquenchable: "Many waters cannot quench love, neither can floods drown it" (v. 7, RSV). It can neither be priced nor purchased: "If a man offered for love all the wealth of his house, it would be utterly scorned" (v. 7, RSV).

What begins as a steady and sober concern for the welfare of another—a sense of responsibility and respect —finds its moving culmination and fitting climax in the dissolving delights of ecstasy. Thus, within the holy bonds of marriage, duty is lifted out of necessity and is transmuted into joy.

In bygone ages marriage was frequently, as in Asia today, a matter of negotiation and arrangements. Parents were responsible for the choice of a bride or bridegroom for their son or daughter. Stephen Neill writes: "Not everyone recognizes how recent and how revolutionary are the views and habits that generally prevail among us with regard to marriage and the choice of a partner. In India, even among Christians, it is almost universally the custom that marriages are arranged by the parents and not by the parties; even today it is no rare event for a college student to be suddenly summoned home to marry a girl whom he has never seen and whom he will not really see until after the marriage ceremony is over. People of education and of modern outlook who defend the ancient custom will maintain that parents who sincerely love their children and carefully consider their character and temperament are much more likely to make a wise choice than young people who are likely to be carried away by the passing excitements of a moment; in support of their case they can point to a large number of highly successful unions in which arranged companionship has passed into deep and abiding affection."[5]

[5] *A Genuinely Human Existence* (London: Constable & Co., Ltd., 1959), p. 182.

Marriages which are based on physical infatuation seldom survive. They lack the sustaining ingredients of mutual regard and common dedication. Physical desire is a fickle, fleeting thing. Easily aroused, it quickly subsides. As Thielicke notes, "pleasure and ecstasy are excitements that rise and fall in definite and steep curves."[6] Every lover wants to prolong the moment of ecstasy. As Nietzsche observes, all pleasure, all joy, "wants eternity—wants deep eternity."[7] but because pleasure is fleeting the cry is always: "Ah, still delay—thou art so fair!"[8] But the moment always passes, to be followed by the inevitable weariness of repletion and the waning of desire.

There is often, associated with the indulgence of lust, a reaction of disgust. A man seeks sexual satisfaction with a prostitute: there is the moment of fierce animal passion and then, as often as not, the revulsion of disgust. Shakespeare comments:

> *The expense of spirit in a waste of shame*
> *Is lust in action . . .*
> *Past reason hunted, and no sooner had*
> *Past reason hated.*[9]

Amnon, after his act of incestuous lust with Tamar, "hated her exceedingly; so that the hatred wherewith he hated her was greater than the love wherewith he had loved her" (II Sam. 13:15). This is the invariable experience of those who enter into marriage "unadvisedly, lightly or wantonly."

This is not to minimize the place of physical passion in the life of man or the reality of erotic pleasure. "An

[6] *Op. cit.,* p. 35.
[7] "Thus Spoke Zarathustra," Walter Kaufmann, ed. and tr., *The Portable Nietzsche* (The Viking Press, Inc., 1954), p. 436.
[8] Goethe, *Faust,* II, V, 6.
[9] *Sonnet* 129.

extremely strong sex urge," Thielicke points out, "can be present in those who, as Christians, subject their sexuality to the discipline of obedience and reverence for one's neighbour."[10] The question, in the ultimate analysis, is whether, as morally responsible beings, we master our sexual desires or are mastered by them; whether our instincts and impulses are permitted to direct us, or are disciplined by us. Christians recognize the reality of sexual desire, but they also recognize that sexual desire is only legitimate when it is subordinated to and controlled by love. Sexual desire, Jesus taught, is to be disciplined and directed: "Ye have heard that it was said by them of old time, Thou shalt not commit adultery: But I say unto you, That whosoever looketh on a woman to lust after her hath committed adultery with her already in his heart" (Matt. 5:27–28). The man who is a seething mass of lustful desire is, Jesus implied, in little better case than the man who commits adultery. The Christian man, for his part, is to bring "into captivity every thought to the obedience of Christ" (II Cor. 10:5).

10 *Op. cit.*, p. 39.

CHAPTER FOUR

MARRIAGE

"A great mystery"

—Eph. 5:32

MARRIAGE, to quote the traditional language of the Prayer Book, "is an honourable estate, instituted of God in the time of man's innocency, signifying unto us the mystical union that is betwixt Christ and his Church." What the preface to the marriage service states, in terms of unambiguous particularity, is that marriage is honorable; that it exists by God's ordination and appointment; that it dates from the time of man's innocency; and that, in a wonderful way, it symbolizes the spiritual union of Christ and the believer.

"For this cause," Jesus said, "shall a man leave father and mother, and shall cleave to his wife: and they twain shall be one flesh?" (Matt. 19:5.) The two sexes, by God's intention and design, belong together. "Neither is the man without the woman, neither the woman without the man, in the Lord." (I Cor. 11:11.) Not only are the two sexes related and directed the one toward the other, in the sexual encounter they become one.

We defame God, and we degrade marriage, when we portray the act of coitus as an unpleasant accommodation to human animality. There is nothing sinful about the estate of marriage. On the contrary, marriage belongs to the original order of creation (Gen. 2:24), and it is, for most men, their appointed role. In his famous wedding sermon, Dietrich Bonhoeffer, writing from his prison cell, says: "Marriage is a kingdom of its own in the midst of the world, a haven of refuge amid the turmoil of our age, nay more, a sanctuary. It is not founded on the shifting sands of private and public life, but has its peace in God. For it is God who gave it its special meaning and dignity, its nature and privilege, its destiny and worth."[1]

Marriage, to quote the Prayer Book again, "is not by any to be enterprised, nor taken in hand, unadvisedly, lightly, or wantonly, to satisfy men's carnal lusts and appetites, like brute beasts that have no understanding; but reverently, discreetly, advisedly, soberly, and in the fear of God." Today, we seldom think of marriage in terms of covenant and vocation; we tend to think of marriage in terms of romance. Of all the motives for marriage, Douglas Rhymes points out, this is the most unstable, the most ephemeral. "The rational and logical outcome of a marriage founded on romance alone," he bluntly insists, "is divorce."[2] This misunderstanding of the nature of marriage would not arise if men and women paid closer attention to "the causes for which Matrimony was ordained."

THE "CAUSES" OF MATRIMONY

The "causes" of marriage are defined in the Prayer Book as parenthood, sexual union, and companionship.

"First, It was ordained for the procreation of children, to be brought up in the fear and nurture of the Lord, and to the praise of his holy Name."

Marriage clearly serves a biological purpose: it is the

[1] *Letters and Papers from Prison* (The Macmillan Company, 1962), p. 151.

[2] *No New Morality: Christian Personal Values and Sexual Morality* (The Bobbs-Merrill Company, Inc., 1964).

means by which the human race is perpetually renewed. The divine commandment is: "Be fruitful, and multiply, and replenish the earth" (Gen. 1:28). Thus God permits man to share derivatively in the work of creation.

The family is the God-given unit not only for the procreation of children but for their care and nurture. "Children," the Bible says, "are a heritage of the Lord" (Ps. 127:3); they are to be brought up "in the nurture and admonition of the Lord" and to the praise of his holy name (Eph. 6:4). Parents are to remember that they are trustees on behalf of God.

Parenthood, then, is one of the primary purposes of marriage.

"Secondly, It was ordained for a remedy against sin, and to avoid fornication; that such persons as have not the gift of continency might marry, and keep themselves undefiled members of Christ's body."

Marriage is the divinely ordained means for the expression of sexual desire. Sexual desire is not, of course, an improper thing, a matter for embarrassed apology; it is, on the contrary, a glorious gift of God for man's delight and sanctification. Sexual desire, however, needs to be disciplined and directed. What is required is an attitude of responsibility and respect; what needs to be avoided is the temptation to lasciviousness. Sexual desire can be a turbulent and destructive tyranny; it can also be a source of perennial delight and creative achievement. The ancient maxim applies: *Abusus non tollit usum,* "Abuse does not bar use." Sex, Christians believe, is a gracious endowment of God. The deposited Prayer Book of 1928 acknowledges that "the natural instincts and affections are implanted by God," but adds that, because of sin, they need "to be hallowed and directed aright."

Negatively speaking, marriage serves a prophylactic purpose: it is "a remedy against sin." As the apostle Paul observes, in his forthright way, "it is better to marry than to burn," or, to quote the more appropriate language of the RSV, "to be aflame with passion" (I Cor. 7:9). "Because of the temptation to immorality," the apostle explains, "each man should have his own wife and each woman her own husband." (V. 2, RSV.) If a man's "passions are strong," he repeats, "and it has to be, let him do as he wishes"; let him marry, "it is no sin" (v. 36, RSV). This does *not* mean that marriage is nothing but "licensed fornication": the apostle is emphatic about enjoining on each partner mutual consideration and concern (vs. 3 f.).

Positively, marriage is the vehicle for the expression of sexual desire. From one point of view it may be spoken of as a safety valve for irresistible desire, but, for the Christian man, it is infinitely more than that—a breathtaking experience (in Barth's words), "a bold and blessed intoxication." In this encounter, we have, Barth says, "the dialectic of difference and affinity, of real dualism and equally real unity, of utter self-recollection and utter transport beyond the bounds of self into union with another, of creation and redemption, of this world and the next."[3]

Intercourse is not only the appropriate means for the expression of love, it is also the means by which love itself is strengthened and sustained. Sexual intercourse is far more than a physical act. "Every human act," Gibson Winter says, "expresses feelings, attitudes, and concerns." Thus we put an arm around a friend in trouble. The physical gesture symbolizes and expresses concern. The same is true of sexual intercourse. The sexual act ex-

[3] *Op. cit.,* p. 120.

presses solidarity, intimacy, and mutual concern. "Sexuality," Winter declares, "without mutual intimacy is counterfeit. It pretends to symbolize attitudes which do not exist." Human acts, however, not only convey attitudes, they also help to create attitudes. "Consequently, sexual intercourse is not simply an expression of intimacy. It is a means of deepening and strengthening intimacy."[4] Thus, Paul warns couples against withholding from each other the obligations of love: "Do not deny yourselves to one another, except when you agree upon a temporary abstinence in order to devote yourselves to prayer; afterwards you may come together again; otherwise, for lack of self-control, you may be tempted by Satan" (I Cor. 7:5, NEB). What matters is mutual consideration: the apostolic principle is that Christians should, by love, serve one another (Gal. 5:13). The husband and wife belong together in a mutuality of loving concern: "the wife hath not power of her own body, but the husband: and likewise also the husband hath not power of his own body, but the wife" (I Cor. 7:4). Thus "the husband should give to his wife her conjugal rights, and likewise the wife to her husband." (V. 3, RSV.) "For this is the will of God," the apostle writes, "your sanctification: that you abstain from immorality; that each one of you know how to take a wife for himself in holiness, and honor, not in the passion of lust like heathen who do not know God." (I Thess. 4:3-5, RSV.)

"Thirdly, It was ordained for the mutual society, help, and comfort, that the one ought to have of the other, both in prosperity and adversity."

Milton, in his celebrated work on divorce, notes that God's first command was not: "Be fruitful and multiply"

---

[4] *Love and Conflict* (Doubleday & Company, Inc., 1958), pp. 100–101.

(the favorite text of Roman apologists); nor was it: "It is better to marry than to burn" (the favorite text, it is alleged, of Protestant apologists); it was rather this: "It is not good for man to be alone." "In God's intention," Milton writes, "a meet and happy conversation is the chiefest and noblest end of marriage." "Loneliness is the first thing which God's eye named not good."[5]

Marriage serves a unitive purpose: "the mutual society, help and comfort which the one ought to have of the other both in prosperity and adversity." Marriage makes companionship possible. It makes possible a relationship in depth, a close and intimate union of heart and mind. "A wise man," Dean Swift avers, in a letter of counsel to a bride, "soon grows weary of acting the lover, and treating his wife like a mistress, but wants a reasonable condition and a true friend through every stage of life. . . . The grand affair of your life," he adds, "will be to gain and preserve the friendship and esteem of your husband."[6]

Concerning procreation, we must say, it will cease; concerning sexual union, it will vanish away; but concerning that fellowship which is the fruit of love, it never fails. As the years go by true marriage becomes an ever-deepening partnership of penitence and privilege, of forgiveness and joy, of suffering and achievement.

Tertullian, in a moving passage (written before his outlook was warped and distorted by Montanism), describes the significance of marriage as a fellowship of faith and love.

"How beautiful, then, the marriage of two Christians, two who are one in hope, one in desire, one in the way of life they follow, one in the religion they practice. They

5 Quoted in Bainton, *op. cit.*, pp. 108–109.
6 Quoted by Mace in *Whom God Hath Joined*, p. 20.

are as brethren, both servants of the same Master.
Nothing divides them, either in flesh or in spirit. They
are, in very truth, *two in one flesh;* and where there is
but one flesh there is also but one spirit. They pray
together, they worship together, they fast together; in-
structing one another, encouraging one another, strengthening one another. Side by side they visit God's church
and partake of God's banquet; side by side they face
difficulties and persecution, share their consolations.
They have no secrets from one another; they never shun
each other's company, they never bring sorrow to each
other's hearts. Unembarrassed they visit the sick and
assist the needy. . . . Psalms and hymns they sing to one
another, striving to see which one of them will chant
more beautifully the praises of their Lord. Hearing and
seeing this, Christ rejoices. To such as these He gives His
peace. Where there are two together, there also He is
present; and where He is, there evil is not."[7]

THE "ORDER" OF MATRIMONY

In Christ, Paul states, "there is neither Jew nor Greek,
there is neither bond nor free, there is neither male nor
female: for ye are all one" (Gal. 3:28). In Christ, he says,
the differences of race and class and sex are transcended
and overcome. But the differences, though transcended,
are not obliterated. Before God there is an equality of
status, but there remains, within marriage, a difference of
function. The husband, by the ordinance of God, is
called to be protector and provider; the wife, by the same
ordinance, mother and homemaker.

Corresponding to the facts of sexual differentiation,
there is, within marriage, a sequence and an order. "The
head of every man is Christ; and the head of the woman

[7] "To His Wife," *Treatises on Marriage and Remarriage*, p. 35.

is the man; and the head of Christ is God." (I Cor. 11:3.)
In this ordered relationship it is man's appointed role to
be both leader and lord. The nature of his lordship is,
however, defined by reference to the work of Christ. "The
husband is the head of the wife, even as Christ is the head
of the church: and he is the saviour of the body. Therefore as the church is subject unto Christ, so let the wives
be to their own husbands in everything. Husbands, love
your wives, even as Christ also loved the church, and gave
himself for it." (Eph. 5:23–25.) When Christ loved the
church he "pleased not himself" (Rom. 15:3); what is
required, within marriage, is a like spirit of willing self-
abnegation. On the occasion of the feet-washing, Jesus
illustrated, by an acted parable, what, within the Christian fellowship, lordship means. "Ye call me Master and
Lord: and ye say well; for so I am. If I then, your Lord
and Master, have washed your feet; ye also ought to wash
one another's feet. For I have given you an example,
that ye should do as I have done to you." (John 13:13–
15.) This is what lordship within marriage means: it
means not aggressive domination but self-forgetful service. It means eager and solicitous concern for the happi-
ness and welfare of the other. The wife, for her part, is to
respond to her husband's loving concern with cheerful
obedience.

The relationship between Christ and the church is
archetypal for Christian marriage. It is to be reflected,
and, insofar as that is possible, reproduced; every man is
to "love his wife even as himself"; and every woman is
"to reverence her husband" (Eph. 5:33).

THE "ESSENCE" OF MATRIMONY

There has been frequent debate as to whether consent
or consummation constitutes the "essence" of marriage.

According to the dictum of Ulpian it is consent, not cohabitation, that makes a marriage. This view was incorporated into the canon law of the church and is reflected in the church's marriage service. The intention of the parties to live together in lifelong fidelity and love is expressed by the public exchange of vows: "Wilt thou have this Woman to thy wedded wife, to live together after God's ordinance in the holy estate of Matrimony? Wilt thou love her, comfort her, honour, and keep her in sickness and in health; and, forsaking all others, keep thee only unto her, so long as ye both shall live?" And the simple, affirmative answer is: "I will." An identical question is then addressed to the bride with the additional requirement of obedience.

The doctrine that consummation makes the marriage, however, has left its mark on both canon law and civil law. Both church and state agree that an unconsummated marriage is no real marriage and may be declared null and void. Nevertheless, the traditional teaching of the church down the ages has been that consent is the true essential. Consummation is the proper consequence of consent: it is the secret ratification and confirmation by the man and the woman of the public "vow and covenant betwixt them made."

There is a helpful comment on what constitutes the "essence" of marriage in the Report of the Commission appointed by the Archbishops of Canterbury and York, entitled *The Church and the Law of Nullity of Marriage* (1955): "From time to time it has been argued that some particular sign, e.g., the joining of hands or the giving of a ring or rings, is of the essence of a form of marriage. The arguments have not found general acceptance in the Church. It has also been argued that the benediction pronounced by the priest before whom the contract is made is of the essence of the form of marriage, or that the priest before whom the marriage takes place is the minister of the sacrament. This is not so. The generally accepted view of Western Christendom has been that the parties are themselves the ministers and that no priestly benediction is necessary for the validity of the marriage."[8]

In the eyes of the law, marriage is fundamentally a contract. That is why the law is concerned that the contracting parties should enter into the contract without duress, freely and willingly, and that there should be no hidden impediments. The congregation, in the introductory part of the service, is charged to make known any "just cause" which might be an impediment to the intended marriage, and the couple are likewise charged, in the most solemn terms, to confess any known impediment.

The couple must not only make the contract; they must be able and willing to carry it out. Willful refusal, like incapacity to consummate, is a legal ground for nullity. Consummation involves, by implication, the procreative end of marriage. That is part of the contract and, in the eyes of the law, must be so regarded. Thus, the Court of Appeal ruled (*Cowen v. Cowen*) that a man who had consistently refused to have intercourse except with a contraceptive device, against the wishes of his wife, had willfully refused to consummate the marriage, thus entitling her to a decree of nullity. Two years later, the judgment was overthrown by the House of Lords. *The Times,* in an editorial, trenchantly criticized the speech of the Lord Chancellor (Lord Jowitt), commenting: "Either bride or bridegroom entering upon marriage with a partner physically capable of parenthood is entitled to presume that this purpose is agreed between them. For one of them deliberately to frustrate the other's desire

8 (London: S.P.C.K., 1955), p. 10.

for children is to do him or her a wrong that goes to the roots of marriage itself."[9] Thus the law has traditionally taken the view that marriage is a contract and that the terms of the contract ought to be fulfilled.

Christians recognize that marriage is more than a legal contract; it is also, they recognize, a solemn covenant. The Roman Church goes farther: it regards marriage as a sacrament. Article XXV, however, points out that marriage is not properly a sacrament, but rather, "a state of life allowed in the Scriptures." Its peculiar dignity is indicated by the fact that Paul speaks of it as "a great mystery" (Eph. 5:32).

"A GREAT MYSTERY"

Ralph Cudworth says that the union in marriage of a man and a woman is more than a mere metaphor or symbol; it is a divinely appointed copy or image of Christ's unity with the church.[10] What constitutes the "mystery" is the fact that the intimate union of marriage reflects the hierarchal relationship which exists between Christ and his church. As Christ is the head, the captain of the unity which he forms with the church, so the husband is, in like manner, the captain, the head of the "one flesh" which he forms with his wife.

Concerning Christ and the church, we sing:

> *From heaven He came and sought her*
> *To be His holy Bride;*
> *With His own blood He bought her,*
> *And for her life He died.*[11]

---

[9] For a detailed discussion, see Norman St. John-Stevas, *Life, Death and the Law* (Indiana University Press, 1961), p. 57.
[10] D. S. Bailey, *The Mystery of Love and Marriage*, p. 112.
[11] S. J. Stone, "The Church's One Foundation."

As Christ loved the church, so he continues to nourish and cherish the church. In like manner, it is the husband's duty, not only to love his wife, but to maintain and cherish her. By doing this, he is, in reality, caring for himself, for she is as his own body (Eph. 5:28).

We may conclude this section by quoting Chrysostom's profound account of what love means in relation to Christian marriage. "Hast thou seen the measure of obedience? hear also the measure of love. Wouldst thou that thy wife should obey thee as the Church doth Christ? have care thyself for her, as Christ for the Church; and if it should be needful that thou shouldst give thy life for her, or be cut to pieces a thousand times, or endure anything whatever, refuse it not; yea, if thou has suffered this thou hast not done what Christ did, for thou doest this for one to whom thou wert already united, but He for her who rejected Him and hated Him. . . . He brought her to His feet by His great care, not by threats nor fear nor any such thing; so do thou conduct thyself towards thy wife."[12]

[12] Quoted by T. K. Abbott in *A Critical and Exegetical Commentary of the Epistles to the Ephesians and to the Colossians,* International Critical Commentary (Edinburgh: T. & T. Clark, 1897), p. 167.

CHAPTER FIVE

DIVORCE

"Except . . . for fornication"

—Matt. 19:9

EMIL BRUNNER writes: "Every State will learn by experience that it cannot allow the divine order of creation to be infringed with impunity. All political anarchy in the State begins with anarchy in marriage. The State in which adultery and divorce are the order of the day is also ripe for political decay. No house can be built with mouldering stones; no sound body can grow out of diseased cells. If the social basis, marriage, is rotten, the whole community is rotten."[1] John Galsworthy makes the succinct observation: "Society is built on marriage—marriage and its consequences."[2]

Over the years there has been a steady increase in the number of divorces (both relatively and absolutely). Dr. David Mace, who is Executive Director of the American Association of Marriage Counselors, draws attention to the fact "that modern marriages are suffering at least a ten percent breakdown rate." "This inevitably means," he gloomily observes, "that each year thousands of new people become disillusioned, and many of them cynical, about the whole business. In these days they do not hesitate to say so, which does not elevate the sanctity of the

[1] *Justice and the Social Order* (London: Lutterworth Press, 1945), p. 127.

[2] *The Forsyte Saga*, quoted by C. M. Chavasse in *Five Questions Before the Church* (London: Canterbury Press, 1947), p. 26.

marriage bond in the public mind." "It is needless," he continues, "to dwell upon the tragic effects upon the children of parents who have failed to manage their relationship with one another." He adds: "To this must be added the tangles which, in these days of indulgent public opinion, result from the liaisons entered into by many who have failed in marriage and consequently find themselves sexually and emotionally frustrated." "This is the feature of the present situation which," he rightly foresees, "is pregnant with disruptive possibilities: the cumulative effect upon society of releasing into it year by year tens of thousands of young people, who, having failed in marriage, must seek to cope with their emotional and sexual needs as best they can."[3]

It has been pointed out that enlarging the grounds of divorce unwittingly tends to promote it. It strengthens the impression that marriage is a trial relationship which can be dissolved if it proves a failure. Couples are encouraged to believe that the way to mend a marriage is to end it.

DIVORCE IN THE BIBLE

"When a man taketh a wife, and marrieth her, then it shall be, if she find no favor in his eyes, because he hath found some unseemly thing in her, that he shall write a bill of divorcement, and give it in her hand, and send her out of his house. And when she is departed out of his house, she may go and be another man's wife." (Deut. 24:1-2, ASV.) Jewish practice recognized the validity of divorce in all cases, but sought to prevent the abuse of easy divorce by moral injunction and judicial regulation. Thus, seen in its historical context, the Mosaic regulation

---

3 *The Outlook for Marriage* (London: The National Marriage Guidance Council, 1946), pp. 10–11.

represented a humane advance on contemporary practice. It set a brake on hasty divorce.

By the time of Christ there was a deep division of opinion between the school of Rabbi Shammai and the school of Rabbi Hillel over the interpretation of the Deuteronomic phrase, "some unseemly thing." The school of Shammai restricted the right of divorce to the case of an unchaste wife; the school of Hillel argued that a husband had the right to divorce his wife for any cause. This was the significance of the question which the Pharisees addressed to Jesus: "Is it lawful," they asked, "for a man to put away his wife for every cause?" (Matt. 19:3.)

If a man's wife was taken in adultery, or convicted of adultery after trial by bitter waters (Num. 5:11 f.), he had no option but to divorce her. Adultery was not an offense that a husband could either condone or forgive. In such circumstances the wife's marriage settlement was also forfeit. Apart from this explicit provision the law recognized the right of a man to divorce his wife at any time. Nevertheless, the law compelling a man to pay back to his wife her dowry when she was divorced discouraged indiscriminate divorce. According to the Mishnah, barrenness over a period of ten years was a ground of divorce, the commandment concerning fruitfulness (Gen. 1:28) being invoked. The rabbis also recognized divorce by mutual consent, the theory being that the consent of the parties was just as essential for the continuance of a marriage as it was for its establishment.

The marriage contract, the prophets taught, is a divine institution and therefore holy. "Therefore take heed to your spirit, and let none deal treacherously against the wife of his youth. For the Lord, the God of Israel, saith that he hateth putting away." (Mal. 2:15–16.)

To the Jews, divorce was always an evil, but a lesser evil than marital infidelity or mutual aversion. Thus the rabbis never opposed divorce for sufficient cause, or by mutual consent.[4]

Jesus, on being asked whether divorce was permissible for "every" cause, replied that Moses permitted divorce by way of concession, because of the hardness of men's hearts (Matt. 19:8). Divorce, however, was not part of the original order of creation. Thielicke comments: "The legal ordinance of divorce is a mark of 'this aeon'; it is definitely *not* an order of creation, but rather—like all law—a regulation of necessity for the fallen world." The marriage laws, Thielicke continues, remain "fundamentally *below* the level of the original institution of marriage." They are relative and provisional; they belong to the life of man as fallen.[5] "In the resurrection," Jesus pointed out, "they neither marry, nor are given in marriage." (Matt. 22:30.) Divorce is an accommodation to the hardness of men's heart's; it does not belong to the life of man as it was meant to be. It is a regulation of necessity for man in his fallen state.

Jesus did not set up a new standard; he reminded men of the original intention of God. For the Christian man there is to be no putting away. He is to fulfill the original intention of God. Paul underlined the Lord's command: "Unto the married I command, yet not I, but the Lord, Let not the wife depart from her husband: but and if she depart, let her remain unmarried, or be reconciled to her husband: and let not the husband put away his wife" (I Cor. 7:10–11).

[4] S. B. Gurewicz, *Divorce in Jewish Law*, Res Judicatae, Vol. 7, No. 4 (Melbourne: The Journal of the Law School).

[5] *Op. cit.*, p. 109.

What, then, does the church mean, when, in the well-known words of the 1920 Lambeth Conference, it defines marriage as "a life-long and indissoluble union for better or for worse of one man with one woman to the exclusion of all others on either side"? The difficulty, as Dr. K. E. Kirk points out, lies in the ambiguity of the word "indissoluble." "It may, of course, mean that marriage 'ought' not to be dissolved, which is the point at issue between the Christian tradition and its critics. But it may also mean that 'marriage cannot be dissolved'—which seems to fly in the face of facts."[6] The question, then, is whether marriage is *ideally* indissoluble or *factually* indissoluble. Is the union of a man and a woman in marriage analogous to the blood relationship of a brother and a sister and therefore, by its very nature, unalterable? But the union of a man and a woman in marriage creates a relationship that is inadmissible to a brother and a sister.

Again, the term "one flesh," it has been argued, necessarily implies permanence. But the apostle uses the same phrase in connection with sexual relations with a prostitute. "Know ye not that he that is joined to a harlot is one body? For, The twain, saith he, shall become one flesh." (I Cor. 6:16, ASV.) No one argues that an immoral relationship of this kind ought not to be dissolved and ought to be perpetuated.

The Lambeth Conference of 1948 came to the conclusion that little was to be gained by the further employment of this term. "We are bound to admit that a union which is indissoluble by divine institution may in fact be wrecked by sin; and that by the sin of one or both partners the personal relationships in marriage can be com-

6 *Marriage and Divorce*, p. 13; quoted by D. S. Bailey in *The Mystery of Love and Marriage*, p. 77.

pletely destroyed. In marriage, therefore, as in other moral issues, the whole history of the Church affords continuous evidence of the conflict between the absolute will of God and the fulfilment of His divine purpose in the face of human fraility."[7] "The Church of England," Archbishop Frederick Temple observed, "does not teach that marriage is indissoluble. It teaches the indissolubility of marriage in the case of those whom God has joined together but it remembers that God separates those who commit adultery."[8]

It is worth examining, at this point, the tradition of the Eastern Church. Eastern tradition holds (as codified in the 117th "novel" of Justinian)[9] that adultery is the "death" of marriage. It destroys the union of "one flesh." All subsequent extensions of the grounds for divorce, in the Orthodox Church, have been based on the same principle that when something happens that is equivalent to the "death" of one or both partners, a marriage may be dissolved. The Orthodox Church now recognizes adultery, apostasy, and desertion over a period of years as legitimate grounds for divorce.

[7] *The Lambeth Conference 1948* (London: S.P.C.K., 1948), p. 98.

[8] *Memoirs.* Quoted by J, Howard Cruse and Bryan S. W. Green in *Marriage, Divorce and Repentance in the Church of England* (London: Hodder & Stoughton, Ltd., 1949), p. 25.

[9] "The revision, enlargement and rearrangement of the Theodosian Code was published by Justinian in 529. It survives only in a revised edition embodying later constitutions which dates from 534. It was supplemented by further constitutions known as 'Novellae' and, in the sphere of case law, by (1) the 'Digest' (533), a comprehensive set of passages from juristic text-books and commentaries of the classical period, and (2) the 'Institutes of Justinian' (533), a revised and modified edition of those of Gaius with extracts from similar works. Together the Code, Novellae, Digest and Institutes constituted the *Corpus Juris Civilis,* which became the authoritative and ordered statement of Roman Law, purged of all that was obsolete or contradictory." F. L. Cross, ed., *The Oxford Dictionary of the Christian Church* (London: Oxford University Press, 1957), p. 757.

The Roman Church is uncompromisingly opposed to divorce on any grounds whatsoever. Nevertheless, there are some who argue that the Roman Church, by stretching causes for annulment, virtually grants divorce under another name. "The Roman Church," H. C. Goudge accuses, "has often permitted divorce in practice by declaring marriages from the first invalid, and that on preposterous grounds."[10] Speaking of the situation as it existed in the pre-Reformation Church, A. T. Macmillan says: "The impediments to marriage arising from consanguinity and affinity, the latter often only theoretical, made it not too difficult, in cases where the marriage was a failure, to obtain a decree of nullity."[11] "The mediaeval system," Mandell Creighton testifies, "was a mass of fictions or dispensations and subterfuges."[12] The Council of Trent invoked the so-called Pauline privilege in justification of the "remarriage" of persons previously married in another church. According to Canon 1126, a former marriage is dissolved by the new "Christian" marriage.

Within the Church of England there has been a progressive hardening of opinion in a rigorist direction. When the Act of 1857 was passed, granting divorce on the ground of adultery, the Act was supported in the House of Lords by the Archbishop of Canterbury, the Bishop of London, and eight other bishops, on the ground that the Act was in accord with Holy Scripture. The Lambeth Conference of 1908 reaffirmed the resolution of the Con-

10 C. Gore, ed., *A New Commentary on Holy Scripture* (The Macmillan Company, 1928), Part III, p. 175.

11 *Marriage, Divorce and the Church* (London: S.P.C.K., 1946), p. 7.

12 Quoted by W. G. Fallows in *Mandell Creighton and the English Church* (London: Oxford University Press, 1964), p. 85.

ference of 1888 in relation to divorce: "That inasmuch as our Lord's words expressly forbid divorce, except in the case of fornication or adultery, the Christian Church cannot recognize divorce in any other than the excepted case, or give any sanction to the marriage of any person who has been divorced contrary to this law, during the life of the other party." In 1935 the Joint Committee of the Convocations, in a report *The Church and Marriage,* reported that "it is the almost unanimous opinion of the scholars consulted that the 'exceptive clause' in Matthew V. 32 and XIX. 9 is in neither place part of the original teaching of our Lord."[13] The Lambeth Conference of 1948 concurred, affirming "that the marriage of one whose former partner is still living may not be celebrated according to the rites of the Church, unless it be established that there exists no marriage bond recognized by the Church."[14]

There are those who argue that what is urgently needed is the establishment of provincial or diocesan nullity courts "to review cases in which a divorce has been granted but, it is contended, a decree of nullity might have been obtained." The Lambeth Conference of 1948 reported that "in the United States, after much thought, new canons have been adopted (1946) under which the bishop is authorized to enquire and decide, in the case of an active member in good standing in the Church whose marriage has been annulled or dissolved by a civil court, that 'no marriage bond as the same is recognized by this Church exists.' " The following Lambeth Conference (1958) commended "for further con-

[13] It needs to be stated emphatically that there are no textual grounds for questioning the authenticity of this passage, and that those who do reject it do so because of prior presuppositions as to what it is assumed our Lord taught.
[14] Resolution 94.

sideration by the Churches and Provinces of the Anglican Communion a procedure for defining marital status, such as already exists in some of its Provinces."

This is the direction in which matters are tending. What are we to say to these things? In 1955 a report entitled *The Church and the Law of Nullity in Marriage* (being the report of a commission appointed by the Archbishops of Canterbury and York in 1949 at the request of the Convocations)[15] affirmed that "no marriage is valid unless mutual consent has been freely given and received," and further agreed that sexual incapacity, mental defect or insanity at the time of the marriage, venereal disease in a communicable form at the time of the marriage, or pregnancy by some other man at the time of the marriage are sufficient grounds for a legal declaration of nullity. The Commission did not, however, feel able to "recommend the establishment of Church Courts to deal with cases of alleged Nullity."

There, in relation to nullity, the matter rests for the time being. The secular courts have tried and accepted procedures for hearing applications for nullity; it is exceedingly doubtful whether the church should seek to intrude into a field where the matters at issue are often delicate questions of medical fact.

It is, however, high time that present policies in relation to divorce were subjected to fresh scrutiny and examination. Does the church, by its practice, demonstrate its belief in the forgiveness of sins? or does the church act as though divorce was the sin for which there is no forgiveness? (Mark 3:29). A casual observer might assume that this is the case.

The late Bishop of Oxford (K. E. Kirk), in *The Vision of God,* draws attention to the fact that there are two contrasted methods of procedure in relation to the ex-

[15] (London: S.P.C.K., 1955.)

ercise of discipline: the one is pastoral and the other is penal. By the former we mean, he says, "such uses of discipline as are designed to comfort, strengthen, and inspire the weakling; by the latter, such usages as have for their purpose to cut off the Church from the world by cutting off the weakling from the Church. It is almost superfluous to ask which of these two methods conforms most closely to the mind of the good Shepherd. He Who broke not the bruised reed, nor quenched the smoking flax, Who consorted with publicans and sinners, Who bade the apostle forgive even to seventy times seven;—whosoever came to Him, though they fell away and came back again time after time, He would in no wise cast out. How He could do this without lowering His standards, abating His demands, or compromising with evil, is His own peculiar secret. The Church must learn it if and as she can; but her best efforts to put it into effect in the face of the complex demands of the world and the specious allurements of the devil have been blundering and blind compared with His."[16]

The church needs to demonstrate that she believes in the possibility of repentance and the reality of God's forgiveness. That is why there are evangelicals who are anxious that the church should be willing to bless those who, after the harrowing tragedy of divorce, are desirous, in penitence and faith, to begin again. It is not without significance that the Eastern Church—whose tradition in this matter is not to be despised—provides an official service in such circumstances. The service includes an act of penitence for the failure of the former marriage, and, for the future, the couple publicly affirm their intention of abiding by the ideals of Christian marriage.

How can we, in this connection, ignore the fact that our Lord himself made an exception in the case of adul-

[16] (London: Longmans, Green & Co., Ltd., 1931), pp. 468–469.

tery? (Matt. 19:9). The apostle Paul recognized that Christians had the right, on conversion, to divorce their pagan partners if they declined to live with them. (Interestingly enough, what Paul permitted, in the old Israel was commanded. In the time of Ezra, the Jews were *compelled* to put away their pagan wives.) The late Bishop of Rochester, C. M. Chavasse, testifies: "I believe that the Orthodox Church has preserved all down the ages of Christendom the true Christian tradition; and that a study of the conception of the 'death' of marriage is long overdue."[17] We commend the statement of the 1948 Lambeth Conference: "On the one hand discipline must not be so rigorous as to exclude from the Church's pastoral care those who have remarried after divorce. On the other hand it must not be so lax as to affront the consciences of Church people, or encourage the idea that divorce does not matter."[18]

THE SITUATION IN AMERICA

The laws that govern the dissolution of marriage in the United States are conflicting and confusing. Dr. David Mace has described it as "an absolutely ghastly, dreadful, deplorably messy situation." A couple may instigate divorce proceedings on forty-seven different grounds, although the grounds differ widely from state to state. All states recognize adultery as a ground for divorce; forty-four, cruelty; forty-seven, desertion; twenty-nine, nonsupport; forty, alcoholism; forty-three, the commission of a felony; and thirty-two, impotence. Unnatural acts, intolerable conduct, insanity, and disease[19] are also recog-

[17] *Five Questions Before the Church* (London: Canterbury Press, 1947), p. 36.
[18] (London: S.P.C.K., 1948), Part II, p. 100.
[19] In Illinois, it is the communication of venereal disease; in Kentucky, concealing or contracting a loathsome disease; in Hawaii, leprosy.

nized in some states. Before its legislature enacted a divorce reform law in April, 1966, New York was the single state recognizing only one ground for divorce, namely, adultery, as proved by third-party testimony. Nevertheless, many New Yorkers found it possible to evade this limiting restriction. Despite the fact that a marriage must be terminated in the state of domicile, it has been found possible in practice to secure a divorce on some less exacting ground by the simple expedient of six weeks' residence in Idaho or Nevada, or a day's residence in Mexico. The New York Court of Appeals, in a notable decision (*Rosenstiel v. Rosenstiel*), recently recognized the validity of Mexican divorce in New York: "A balanced public policy requires," the court ruled, "that recognition of the bilateral Mexican divorce be given rather than withheld." It is significant that no less than 250,000 New Yorkers have secured Mexican divorces.

It has been mordantly stated that Americans appear to be marrying more and enjoying it less. Approximately 400,000 couples are divorced each year: more than 6,000,-000 Americans are divorced or separated. Forty-six percent of all divorces involve girls who marry in their teens, and 74 percent those who marry under twenty-five.

To the couples involved, *Time* magazine editorialized,[20] "a marital breakup is an intensely personal affair, full of anguish, doubt and a sense of failure." That is why eighteen states have created what are called "conciliation courts." These courts attempt to mend marriages with the aid of full-time staff psychologists and social workers. The courts claim to have successfully saved 43 percent of the cases voluntarily brought before them. Christians can only applaud constructive measures of this kind designed to preserve and strengthen the institution of marriage.

[20] February 11, 1966.

CHAPTER SIX

PROMISCUITY

"Eyes full of adultery"

—II Peter 2:14

THERE is, says Roger Shinn, a new attitude toward sex in the United States. The old slogan, "Beware of sex," has been replaced, he suggests, by a new slogan "Hurrah for sex."[1] The phenomenal popularity of *Playboy* magazine is sufficient proof of the truth of this observation.

Nevertheless, there is another side to the coin. "In the United States," Roger Shinn observes, "more than 250,000 babies are born to unmarried mothers each year, and about 1 out of 5 brides is pregnant at her wedding. Estimates of illegal abortions in the United States range from 200,000 to one million; perhaps 1 out of 4 pregnancies ends in abortion."[2]

In England a similar situation exists. In 1964 a Committee of the British Medical Association published a disturbing report entitled *The Problem of Venereal Disease, Particularly Among Young People.*[3]

The statistical facts indicate the nature of the problem. During the years 1951–1962 the population of England and Wales increased by 6.5 percent and the incidence of sexually transmitted disease by 73.5 percent. These statistics do not, however, include patients who were treated

[1] *Tangled World* (Charles Scribner's Sons, 1965), p. 133.
[2] *Ibid.*, p. 131.
[3] Published by the British Medical Association, March, 1964.

outside the National Health Service, those treated by general practitioners who were not referred to clinics, and those who were treated by medical officers in the Armed Services. If these additional categories are included, the figure of 73.5 percent would be higher still.

The committee found that there had been a steep *down* trend in the figures for gonorrhea from 1947 to 1951 (due to improved drug therapy), but, since 1951, the committee noted that the trend had been "decisively reversed."

During the period, 1957–1961, gonorrhea increased among males (per 10,000 of the population) 48.6 percent; among the age group 15–24, 62.9 percent. For the female population the figures, however, are substantially higher, the increase for females (per 10,000 of the population) being 65.1 percent, and for the age group 15–24, 78.0 percent. The committee pointed out that what these figures indicate is not only a marked increase in the actual incidence of gonorrhea (despite the availability of drugs and contraceptive devices) but, even more disturbingly, a marked increase in teen-age promiscuity and infection.

There are those who would like to adopt the flattering fiction that it is the colored migrants, who have entered Britain since the end of World War II, who are chiefly responsible for the spread of venereal infection. The committee rejected this face-saving hypothesis. There are, the committee noted, two main charges: "The first is the often-repeated assertion that immigrants are largely responsible for the rise in venereal diseases. The second is the allied statement that morals are more lax and promiscuity more rife among colored people than white." The committee found that, outside London, and four or five other large cities, "venereal disease in immigrants is virtually a non-existent problem." In Scotland, for example, 86.6 percent of the male patients and 98.7 percent of the female patients were persons who had been born in the United Kingdom. The accusation, therefore, that colored migrants are mainly responsible for the dramatic increase in the incidence of venereal disease does not bear close examination.[4]

The committee drew attention to another disturbing fact. Homosexual activity is, they discovered, a contributing factor to the increasing incidence of venereal disease. In some clinics (according to the testimony of the British Co-operative Clinical Group) 50 percent or more of new cases of primary and secondary syphilis occur in male homosexuals.

The evidence for increased promiscuity is to be found, the committee noted, not only in the rising incidence of venereal disease but also in the number of illegitimate maternities. Now two out of three babies, born to girls under twenty years of age, are conceived out of wedlock, and the total number of such births, the committee pointed out, has doubled between 1948 and 1961. This does not take into account the number of those who, having become pregnant, have resorted to abortion.

"AN UNDERLYING MALAISE"

These things are symptomatic, the committee said, "of an underlying malaise affecting the social and sexual life of a society." There is, they said, "a radically altered attitude towards sexual morality, and morality in general." "It is difficult to decide," they commented, "how far the 'Bomb' is to be blamed for the intellectual restlessness and moral laxity which older people see among the young of today. Some witnesses put it to us that the fear of world annihilation was the direct cause of a desperate search for

[4] *Ibid.,* pp. 23–24.

pleasure, and a desire to sample all the physical sensations that life has to offer before it is too late. One witness, the organizer of a youth club in a small country town, asked the club's members what they would do if they were told that nuclear war was imminent. Said one boy: 'Sleep with Brenda.' "[5]

The representatives of the angry young men in England, and of the beat generation in America, hysterically proclaim that "marriage . . . becomes form without substance in an age where tomorrow has a horizon darkened by a mushroom cloud." In these apocalyptic times, "all of life becomes an accumulation of ends, with all goals immediate,"[6] a feverish pursuit of "kicks," a search for what Norman Mailer calls "an orgasm more apocalyptic than the one which preceded it."[7]

Of course there is nothing new in all this. It is simply the ancient philosophy of hedonism refurbished and renewed. It is the philosophy which says: "Let us eat and drink, for tomorrow we die" (I Cor. 15:32).

"NECKING AND PETTING"

In the sophisticated countries of the West there is, among teen-agers, a compulsive urge to sexual experimentation. This finds expression in the cult of necking and petting. (It is a campus convention to use the word "necking" for the neck up; "petting" for more extensive bodily contacts.) Both necking and petting involve the deliberate pursuit of erotic excitation. The argument is sometimes advanced that these activities are permissible because they do not, as a rule, involve the full act of intercourse. They

---

[5] Ibid., p. 34.
[6] Gene Feldman and Max Gartenberg, eds., The Beat Generation and the Angry Young Men (Dell Publishing Co., Inc., 1959), p. 12.
[7] Ibid., p. 382.

do not necessarily involve the violation of technical virginity. Concerning this argument the editors of the volume, *Sex and the Church,* prepared by the Family Life Committee of the Lutheran Church—Missouri Synod, say: "The excuse that it avoids intercourse and preserves the girl's virginity is a moral subterfuge since the integrity of another person is violated. . . . Petting cheapens sex. . . . It often results in nervous tensions, feelings of indignity, resentfulness, hypocrisy. Petting experiences are stored in the conscious mind to plague and disturb. It is difficult to stop the demands for progressively increasing sex stimulation. Petting becomes a Frankenstein which the creator can no longer manage. . . . Selfhood is exploited in heavy petting, and self-respect forfeited."[8]

THE KINSEY REPORTS

It is not possible to discuss the present-day state of sexual morality without reference to the significance of the statistical material collected and collated by Dr. Kinsey in his epoch-making studies, *Sexual Behaviour in the Human Male*[9] and *Sexual Behaviour in the Human Female.*[10] Dr. Kinsey's studies confirm the fact (if confirmation is necessary) that there is widespread sexual lawlessness. We are not concerned to question the accuracy of Dr. Kinsey's statistics; but we may question the validity of Dr. Kinsey's behavioristic presuppositions. In relation to premarital intercourse, Dr. Kinsey writes: "The fact that the single male, from adolescence to 30 years of age, does have a frequency of nearly 3.0 per week, is evidence of the ineffectiveness of social restrictions and the imperativeness of the biologic demands. For those

8 *Op. cit.,* p. 154.
9 (W. B. Saunders Company, 1948).
10 (W. B. Saunders Company, 1953).

who like the term, it is clear that there is a sexual drive which cannot be set aside for any large portion of the population, by any sort of social convention."[11]

The late Dr. Kinsey was a professional zoologist: he applied to the study of the human male and female the statistical methods which he used so successfully in the study of gall wasps. He was unable to see, however, that sexuality in man is something different from sexuality in animals, and that, for human beings, there is a fundamental distinction between what a man *can* do and what he *ought* to do. Dr. Kinsey disclaimed the role of a moralist: he was, he insisted, a scientist and nothing more. Nevertheless, as Geoffrey Gorer points out, "behind the mask of dispassionateness, you can easily discern Dr. Kinsey's astonished admiration for the people with the larger rates of 'outlet' and his contemptuous pity for those making poor scores." Geoffrey Gorer continues: "A little anthropological knowledge might have rectified this attitude. We have information from enough primitive societies to suggest that there is an (apparently) direct correlation between high rates of intercourse and lack of emotional interest in sex or belief in love." "For a society that believes in love," he says, "be it sacred or profane, the physiological aspect of love cannot be separated from the emotional and psychological concomitants without reducing it to meaninglessness."[12]

No one can read the reports without noting Dr. Kinsey's references to what he terms "normal" sexual behavior. We ought to regard sex, he says, as "a normal biologic function, acceptable in whatever form it is manifested."[13] The question that we must ask is this: Is

11 *Sexual Behaviour in the Human Male,* p. 269.
12 *The American Scholar,* Summer, 1948.
13 *Op. cit.,* p. 263.

"normal" behavior the statistical average, or is it that which is in harmony with the true nature of man as a self-determining and morally responsible human being? Again and again Dr. Kinsey makes pejorative judgments about traditional morality: he equates what is "average" with what is "normal" and he implies that what is "normal" is what is "right." It is the "biologic," he says, which should determine moral conduct and behavior.[14]

Millicent McIntosh, in a symposium that seeks to analyze and evaluate the findings of Dr. Kinsey, says that "the Kinsey Report uses all the techniques to which Americans are especially vulnerable. Its pages and pages of statistics, while dull and very depressing, are equally impressive to the ordinary person." She points out how easily a person's defenses can be broken down by the unscrupulous manipulation of these statistics.

All boys and girls are pathetically anxious to be "normal." . . . They are especially vulnerable in the whole area of boy-girl relationships. Whatever is done by the crowd is what they must do, lest they risk being peculiar, blue stocking, prudish, with the inevitable result of unpopularity. So if the Kinsey Report announces that ninety-one percent of females have done petting by the age of twenty-five, and eighty-one percent by the age of eighteen, the girl who is being pressed by a boy to go further than she thinks proper feels herself trapped by these statistics. If she is not erotically aroused, or does not wish to be, she begins to wonder if she is normal.[15]

The difficulty arises from the acceptance of the unspoken but implied assumption that what everyone does we may

[14] Dr. Kinsey frankly adds: "By English and American standards such an attitude is considered primitive, materialistic or animalistic, and beneath the dignity of a civilized and educated people." *Sexual Behaviour in the Human Male*, p. 263.

[15] D. P. Geddes, ed., *An Analysis of the Kinsey Reports on Sexual Behaviour in the Human Male and Female* (Mentor Book, New American Library of World Literature, Inc., 1954), pp. 139-140.

do, indeed ought to do. A university counselor stated that many college boys felt that they were not actually virile if they could not keep up with the statistics Dr. Kinsey presents of sex experience for males of their age.

The Christian, however, has an entirely different point of reference and a different understanding of what maturity means. God, the apostle says, has given us "a spirit of power and love and self-control" (II Tim. 1:7, RSV).

THE "PLAYBOY PHILOSOPHY"

No account of the contemporary scene is complete without some discussion of what is called the *"Playboy* Philosophy." *"Playboy,"* Hugh Hefner explains, "naturally includes sex as one of the ingredients in its total entertainment and service package for the young urban male." "A good men's magazine," he believes, "should include *both* fine fiction and pictures of beautiful girls with 'plunging necklines or no necklines at all' . . . because most normal men will *enjoy* both, and both fit into the concept of a sophisticated urban men's magazine."[16]

No one can deny the nature of Hefner's publishing achievement (he claims a printing of almost two million copies for each issue) or the photographic excellence of the layout. We may concur that "there is still a substantial amount of sick, sin-laden and sensational sex available in every medium of mass communication here in the United States," and that we need "to accept sex more simply and honestly, as a natural part of human experience."

Hefner quotes Kinsey's impressive statistics for extramarital sexual activity, and then comments: "The extent

16 *The Playboy Philosophy* (HMH Publishing Co., Inc., 1962). Hugh Hefner has reprinted a series of eighteen editorials which are now available in documentary form. Unfortunately, pagination is missing.

and variety of human sexual behavior is now an established scientific fact, widely published and well pub-
licized. Whenever a person is now arrested, tried, or
convicted for committing a sexual act of the kind we
have been discussing here (acts treated by the laws of the
land as immoral or perverse) those in authority are
blatantly ignoring the evidence that a majority of our
society regularly engages in similar activity." And then
he adds, defiantly: "Either imprison all of us—or none
of us."

Two comments may be made. First, the fact that people
indulge in certain behavior does not necessarily make
that behavior right. Most people have, at some time or
other, told a lie; the universality of the phenomena does
not make the practice of lying right. Most people who
drive a car have, at some time or other, broken the speed
limit; this fact does not, in itself, justify the removal of
all restrictions relating to driving. The morality or right-
ness of certain kinds of behavior must be established by
relation to criteria other than that of statistical incidence.

Second, sexual activity only becomes fully satisfying
and meaningful when it takes place in the context of
love. Most men, Hefner says, find women seductively
attractive, but they are not, as he likes to think, simply
"Bunnies": they are persons, not playthings. Harvey Cox
points out that "the most famous feature of the magazine
is its monthly fold out photo of a *playmate*. She is
the symbol par excellence of recreational sex. . . . As the
crew-cut young man in a *Playboy* cartoon says to the
rumpled and disarrayed girl he is passionately embracing,
'Why speak of love at a time like this?' "

Hefner agrees that "sex is, at its best, an expression of
love and adoration." "But," he cautions, "this is not to
say that sex is, or should be, limited to love alone." "Sex,"

68

he insists ("with or without love"), "can be one of the most profound and rewarding elements in the adventure of living."

This is the basic question at issue: Is sex, not only with love but without love, a legitimate activity and a proper pursuit?[17] It needs to be said emphatically, by way of reply, that sex without love is lust, and that, to use another person as a mere instrument of physical gratification, is exploitation. What is so conspicuously absent from Hefner's hedonistic interpretation of sex is the Biblical concept of "sanctification and honor." For Christians the sexual relationship is fundamentally personal. It symbolizes, and it strengthens, an already existing relationship of heart and mind. Within this context of full and free personal commitment, love gives to sex its sanctity and significance.

Hefner has a very different understanding of the role of sex in the life of man. Chastity, he bluntly asserts, is just another word for repression; repression is harmful; anyone who knowingly inflicts harm on another—including himself—is cruel; and cruelty is immoral. Let us not be deceived by words: behind the mask of cultured sophistication, what we are being offered is license to sin. On closer examination what purports to be a "philosophy" proves to be the doctrine of sexual permissiveness and the cult of physical gratification.

THE NEED FOR SELF-DISCIPLINE

For all young people the demands of sex are urgent and imperious. Nevertheless, the Scriptural injunction is unambiguous: "Keep thyself pure" (I Tim. 5:22). In rela-

17 Hefner writes: "We recognize that sex without love exists; that it is not in itself, evil; and that it may sometimes serve a definitely worthwhile end."

tion to sexual immorality the apostolic injunction is blunt and urgent: "Flee fornication" (I Cor. 6:18).

What this means in the concrete situation may be illustrated by reference to the experience of Joseph recorded in the pages of the Old Testament. Potiphar's wife found Joseph sexually desirable and she persistently sought to seduce him. Joseph repelled her advances: "My master has no concern about anything in the house, and he has put everything that he has in my hand; . . . nor has he kept back anything from me except yourself, because you are his wife; how then can I do this great wickedness, and sin against God?" (Gen. 39:8–9, RSV.) Nevertheless, she was not abashed. She awaited a convenient opportunity, and then she caught him, seeking his compliance: Joseph did not argue or delay, but got himself out and fled.

Joseph, in resisting the solicitation to evil, was not moved by prudential considerations of self-preservation: he was not concerned that he might be discovered and punished; it was simply that to do this thing would be to sin against God.

David was tempted, in like manner, to sexual self-indulgence. Where Joseph resisted, David succumbed. He allowed himself to be captivated by the alluring beauty of Bathsheba, the wife of Uriah the Hittite (II Sam. 11:2 f.). After the commission of his sin, the prophet Nathan was sent by God to rebuke the king. David saw the enormity of his offense. In penitent prayer he poured out his heart to God. "Against thee, thee only, have I sinned, and done this evil in thy sight." (Ps. 51:4.) He had sinned against Uriah and against Bathsheba, his wife, but he saw that, in the last analysis, it was God against whom he had sinned.

It is the vertical dimension that is so conspicuously

missing from the modern mind. The best preservative from temptation, today as always, is a saving recollection of God. It is at God's tribunal that we must one day stand to give an account of that which we have done in the body, whether it be good or bad (II Cor. 5:10).

Christians will therefore avoid every inducement to sin; they will shun situations of special temptation. (Christians, for example, will recognize the dangers inseparable from prolonged and protracted "petting" sessions.) What is required is a realistic recognition of the dangers of invited temptation, and a sensible avoidance of premature sexual stimulation.

The Christian attitude to sex is, above all, one of reverent responsibility. Christians do not joke about sex, William Temple said, for the same reason that they do not joke about the Sacrament of Holy Communion: it is not that sex is nasty, but that sex is sacred, and to joke about it is profanity.[18] Sex is a God-given endowment to be kept in trust for the beloved, that person to whom one is able to offer oneself in the glad and responsible union of lifelong marriage.

18 *The Church Looks Forward* (London: Macmillan & Co., Ltd., 1944), p. 75.

CHAPTER SEVEN

HOMOSEXUALITY

"Going after strange flesh"

—Jude 7

THE SUBJECT of homosexuality has enjoyed an unenviable notoriety since Dr. Kinsey, in *Sexual Behaviour in the Human Male,* revealed that 37 percent of the male population of the United States has some form of homosexual experience leading to orgasm between the beginning of adolescence and old age.[1] Four percent of all males, he claimed, after the onset of adolescence, are exclusively homosexual throughout their lives.[2]

In England, as the result of a celebrated trial, which dramatically focused attention on the problem, a special departmental committee was appointed under the chairmanship of Sir John Wolfenden. The report of the committee appeared in 1957.[3]

In the meantime, some English Quakers, having been approached by some students who were faced with homosexual difficulties, requesting help and guidance, undertook an independent study. The result of their deliberations was published in a booklet entitled *Towards a Quaker View of Sex.*[4] These Quakers expressed the view that homosexuality is no more blameworthy than left-

[1] P. 623.
[2] P. 651.
[3] *Report of the Committee on Homosexual Offences and Prostitution* (London: Her Majesty's Stationery Office, 1957.)
[4] (London: Friends' House, 1963).

handedness.[5] We ought, they said, to rid ourselves of the view that homosexual behavior is necessarily sinful. "Motive and circumstances degrade or ennoble any act, and we feel that to list sexual acts as sins is to follow the letter rather than the spirit, to kill rather than to give life."[6] "Morals," they argued, "like the Sabbath, were made for man, not man for morals."[7] "We see no reason why the physical nature of a sexual act should be the criterion by which the question whether or not it is moral should be decided. An act which expresses true affection between two individuals and gives pleasure to them both, does not seem to us to be sinful by reason *alone* of the fact that it is homosexual."[8]

THE HOMOSEXUAL CONDITION

There is voluminous literature on the subject of homosexuality and its presumed causation. A primary distinction needs to be made, however, between transient homosexuality and sex inversion. Human beings, in their progress from childhood to maturity, appear to pass through a stage of relative homosexuality, from which the transition is made to heterosexuality. Some, however, fail to make this transition, and become inverts. Inversion is the diversion of the psychosexual impulse more or less exclusively toward persons of the same sex by those who should have reached psychosexual maturity. (Perverts, by contrast, are persons who have turned to homosexual practices and who have no such determined condition.)

There are those who regard homosexuality as a congenital anomaly. Others regard it as a psychogenetically acquired misdirection of the sexual impulse. In this

5 P. 26.
6 P. 41.
7 P. 12.
8 P. 41.

73

connection the Freudians tend to interpret it as a failure to resolve the Oedipus complex; the Adlerians, as a manifestation of inferiority in the case of men who distrust their own virility and ability to dominate the opposite sex; yet others, as the consequence of a traumatic experience in early years.

Norman St. John-Stevas, in a wise and humane discussion (*Life, Death and the Law*),[9] notes that both Paul and Augustine imply that homosexual sins are a *recompense* for other sins, the result of a wider sinfulness and an abandonment of moral standards. "These views," he adds, "have been strikingly confirmed by contemporary research workers, for, in many, although not all, homosexual 'case' histories, there is a background of parental divorce, separation, or estrangement."[10] "One of the most frequent predisposing or precipitating causes of inversion," according to the report, *Sexual Offenders and Social Punishment,* "is an unsatisfactory emotional adjustment in childhood."[11]

Prior to 1861 the penalty for homosexuality was death, but after 1861, a period of penal servitude from ten years to life was substituted. Today, the usual punishment is imprisonment. "From the point of view of cure," St. John-Stevas says, "it is as futile as hoping to rehabilitate a chronic alcoholic by giving him occupational therapy in a brewery."[12] Sir Robert Boothby (now Lord Boothby), in a House of Commons debate, accused: "Our prisons are today, in their overcrowded condition, factories for the manufacture of homosexuality."[13]

9 (Indiana University Press, 1961).

10 P. 215.

11 (London: Church Information Board, 1956), p. 29.

12 *Op. cit.*, p. 225.

13 House of Commons Debate, April 28, 1954. Quoted by J. Tudor Rees and Harley V. Usill, eds., in *They Stand Apart* (London: William Heineman, Ltd., 1955), p. 208.

Homosexual acts between males in America, as in England, are criminal offenses. Nevertheless, there are, in practice, considerable differences between states. Certain states, such as Arkansas, punish only sodomy, and this is strictly defined. Vermont is unique in *not* punishing sodomy. The American Law Institute, like the British Wolfenden Report, has recommended, in its model code, that sexual relations of a homosexual nature between consenting adults should no longer be subject to law, provided they take place in private. So far there has been little attempt to implement the recommendations of the American Law Institute (except in Illinois), although in some states maximum penalties have been reduced. However, others have made their penalties more severe. Evidence of homosexuality automatically precludes a man from military service; and a single homosexual act by any member of the United States Armed Forces is sufficient cause for a dishonorable discharge.

There is little evidence to suggest that it is possible to reorient a true invert—despite the claims of some psychoanalysts. Freud, writing to the mother of a homosexual, said: "In general we cannot promise to achieve cure. In a certain number of cases we succeed in developing the blighted germs of heterosexual tendencies which are present in every homosexual. In the majority of cases it is no more possible. It is a question of the quality and age of the individual. The result of treatment cannot be predicted."[14]

Some Scandinavian countries have resorted to castration (either voluntary or compulsory) as a means by which to treat sexual offenders. Johan Bremer, the Medical Director of the Gaustad Mental Hospital in Oslo, who made a follow-up study of 244 cases, reported that many patients were "dissatisfied, embittered and full of

14 Quoted in Rees and Usill, *op. cit.*, p. 126.

hatred on account of castration."[15] The Wolfenden Report summarily rejected castration as a remedy,[16] and a Roman Catholic Committee commenting on the proposal, expressed its "abhorrence."[17]

A less drastic method of medical treatment is the administration of hormones to diminish the intensity of the sexual drive. While diminishing the drive, this does not cure the condition.

DISEASE OR CRIME?

Humanitarians argue that we should think in terms of disease rather than crime and urge that what is required is treatment rather than punishment. There are others, however, who passionately reject this view. "I believe," C. S. Lewis trenchantly observes, "that the 'humanity' which it claims is a dangerous illusion and disguises the possibility of cruelty and injustice without end."[18] Psychiatric treatment under a court order may not be called "punishment," he notes, it may be called healing. "But do not let us be deceived by a name. To be taken without consent from my home and friends; to lose my liberty; to undergo all those assaults on my personality which modern psychotherapy knows how to deliver; to be re-made after some pattern of 'normality' hatched in a Viennese laboratory to which I never professed allegiance; to know that this process will never end until either my captors have succeeded or I grown wise enough to cheat them with apparent success—who cares whether this is called Punishment or not?"[19]

[15] *Asexualization* (The Macmillan Company, 1959), p. 26.
[16] *Op. cit.*, p. 72.
[17] *Dublin Review*, Roman Catholic Report, Summer, 1956, p. 64.
[18] "The Humanitarian Theory of Punishment," *The Churchman*, June, 1959, p. 55.
[19] *Ibid.*, p. 57.

We are far too ready, he suggests, to discard the traditional doctrine of personal responsibility on which our penal system is based. The concept of retributive punishment presupposes, he says, the concept of desert. It is based on a profound and ineradicable belief in the doctrine of moral responsibility.

Barbara Wootton continues the debate in an article entitled "Sickness or Sin?" "The concept of illness," she pointedly comments, "expands continually at the expense of the concept of moral failure."[20] Dr. Bernard Glueck, the Supervising Psychiatrist at Sing Sing Prison, she notes, has said that we ought to eliminate the concept of criminal responsibility, substituting the concept of "the anti-social individual" as a "sick person, in need of treatment rather than punishment."[21] The identification of the sinful with the sick, she observes, is likely to mark "the final victory of medicine over morals." "Indeed the end of all moral judgment is in sight,"[22] she gloomily observes.

Are homosexual acts a sign of criminality? Or of sickness? This debate is of immediate relevance in relation to the problem of homosexuality. There are those who argue that homosexual acts are crimes to be punished by the full severity of the law; and there are those who argue that homosexual acts are evidence of maladaptive behavior needing psychiatric therapy.

The Wolfenden Report, acknowledging that "there exists in certain persons a homosexual propensity," urged "that homosexual behaviour between consenting adults in private should no longer be a criminal offence."[23] "We

20 *The Twentieth Century*, May, 1956, p. 434.
21 *Ibid.*, p. 437.
22 *Ibid.*, p. 438.
23 *Op. cit.*, p. 25.

do not think," the committee stated, "that it is proper for the law to concern itself with what a man does in private unless it can be shown to be so contrary to the public good that the law ought to intervene in its function as the guardian of that public good."[24] Again, "unless a deliberate attempt is to be made by society, acting through the agency of the law, to equate the sphere of crime with that of sin, there must remain a realm of private morality and immorality which is, in brief and crude terms, not the law's business. To say this is not to condone or encourage private immorality. On the contrary, to emphasize the personal and private nature of moral or immoral conduct is to emphasize the personal and private responsibility of the individual for his own actions, and that is a responsibility which a mature agent can properly be expected to carry for himself without the threat of punishment from the law."[25]

"Where adultery, fornication and lesbian behaviour are not criminal offences there seems to us," the committee continued, "to be no valid ground, on the basis of damage to the family, for so regarding homosexual behaviour between men."[26] The committee, however, insisted that acts of violence, assault, or the seduction of minors, should continue to be criminal offenses.

The Church of England Moral Welfare Council, in a report *Sexual Offenders and Social Punishment,* was concerned to stress that inversion—the homosexual condition—is not, itself, sinful.[27] The council agreed with the recommendation of the Wolfenden Report that homosexual acts in private between consenting adults should

24 *Ibid.,* p. 21.
25 *Ibid.,* p. 24.
26 *Ibid.,* p. 22.
27 P. 27.

no longer be a criminal offense. "We would reiterate emphatically that this plea for justice and legal consistency in no way involves the slightest mitigation of the Church's condemnation of sin and of moral evil. Nor does it imply an indifference to the welfare of society. Nevertheless we have kept in mind the Church's duty to see, insofar as may lie in its power, that all men and women receive equal and impartial treatment at the hands of the law, and that individual freedom is not unduly threatened. We do not believe that the ends of morality can ever be served by connivance at injustice."[28] The council noted, as further evils, the number of suicides caused by the existing law; the opportunities created for blackmail and police corruption; the creation of an aggrieved and self-conscious minority. "To distinguish, as we have done," the council repeated, "between condition and conduct, and to plead for sympathy and help for the invert, does not mean that his anti-social conduct must be condoned or excused."[29]

The Bible condemns impartially all sexual license. Under the Mosaic law the man who committed adultery was liable to the death penalty (Lev. 20:10); in like manner, the man who committed the abomination of the Egyptians and the Canaanites by lying with mankind as with womankind was also liable, under the Mosaic law, to the death penalty (chs. 18:22; 20:13). Paul, denouncing the profligacy of the Roman world, speaks of those who, "leaving the natural use of the woman, burned in their lust one toward another; men with men working that which is unseemly" (Rom. 1:27). Augustine condemns "shameful acts against nature"[30] and Thomas Aquinas

[28] P. 15.
[29] P. 36.
[30] *The City of God*, III. xvi. 30.

79

points out that homosexual acts are inconsistent with right reason. The moral act, he affirms, is one that is consonant with right reason, being directed to its proper end in a fitting manner. In the case of the venereal act the proper end is procreation, and the fitting manner is the "natural method" of heterosexual coitus. Every homosexual act between males is "against nature" and inconsistent with right reason, since it necessarily involves the pursuit of venereal pleasure in such a way as to exclude the possibility of generation.[31]

The genuine invert, however, is tempted to argue that since he is such by the will of God, he ought to be permitted this "natural" mode of expression. Canon Douglas Rhymes, preaching in Southwark Cathedral on March 10, 1963, declared: "Much of the prejudice against homosexuality is on the ground that it is unnatural—unnatural for whom? Certainly not for the homosexual himself."[32] But this kind of reasoning is as misleading as it is mischievous. Sherwin Bailey rightly replies that "inversion can no more be regarded as God's will for a person than can, for example, deformity or mental deficiency." The invert, he says, is "an anomaly whose sexual disorientation bears its own tragic witness to the disordering of humanity by sin." "Sympathy with the homosexual's predicament," he continues, "cannot alter the fact that his practices, though congruent with his condition, are objectively unnatural and cannot reasonably be regarded otherwise."[33]

---

[31] *Summa Theologica,* II-II, q. 153, art. 2; q. 154, arts. 1, 11, and 12.
[32] Quoted by Arnold Lunn and Garth Lean in *The New Morality* (London: Blandford Press, Ltd., 1964), p. 84.
[33] "The Homosexual and Christian Morals," *They Stand Apart,* p. 50.

Oscar Wilde flippantly observed that the easiest way to get rid of a temptation is to yield to it.[34] As Oscar Wilde discovered, to his cost, this is the way to damnation and ruin.

There is, however, another way: the way of steadfast reliance on the grace of God. The homosexual, whose condition is apparently incurable, must humbly and penitently accept his condition and offer it up to God. Paul was burdened with a grievous malady which he calls "a thorn in the flesh"; three times he prayed for deliverance; his prayer was answered, but the thorn remained: "My grace," God said, "is sufficient for thee: for my strength is made perfect in weakness" (II Cor. 12:9). The person whose homosexuality is deep-seated and chronic and apparently incurable need not despair: God's grace is all-sufficient. To quote an Interim Report produced by a group of Anglican clergy and doctors for private circulation: "It is a matter of Christian experience that faithful acceptance of a difficult way of life in response to a moral demand always finds reinforcement in a powerful movement from God towards man."[35]

The Christian man who finds himself afflicted with the heavy burden of a homosexual disposition must seek to sublimate his homosexuality in constructive and creative service; he must studiously avoid "occasions for sin" knowing the awful dangers of invited temptation; he must continue to offer up prayers and supplications with strong crying and tears unto him that is able to save him from death, knowing that he will be heard (Heb. 5:7).

[34] *Picture of Dorian Gray* (1891), Ch. 2.
[35] *The Problem of Homosexuality* (London: Church Information Board, n.d.), p. 15.

CHAPTER EIGHT

THE "NEW" MORALITY

"These . . . despise dominion"
—Jude 8

BISHOP ROBINSON complains (in *Christian Morals Today*) that "the phrase 'the new morality' is bandied about in the wildest manner" and that the term "has become an indiscriminate target of abuse among churchmen." "It might," he testily observes, "be worth just interjecting a historical note to restore a bit of proportion. In the first place, of course, it is not my phrase at all, but the Pope's —or rather that of the Supreme Sacred Congregation of the Holy Office. It had in origin nothing to do with sex, but with existentialist or 'situational' ethics."[1] The Holy Office, however, was not responsible for coining the phrase. It was minted long before. G. E. Newsom, Master of Selwyn College, Cambridge, in 1932, published a book called *The New Morality*,[2] and in 1943, David Mace, in a book, *Does Sex Morality Matter?*[3] entitled a chapter, "The New Morality." (Both Newsom and Mace were concerned to refute a controversial book by Bertrand Russell called *Marriage and Morals*.[4]) That former controversy, however, had little to do with the present debate, to which we now turn.

[1] (The Westminster Press, 1964), p. 8.
[2] (London: Ivor, Nicholson and Watson, 1932).
[3] (London: Rich & Cowan, 1943).
[4] Bertrand Russell explained that his desire was "to cleanse sex from the filth with which it has been covered by Christian moralists."

When Bishop Robinson appeared as a witness for the defense in the case of *Lady Chatterley's Lover* he was asked whether D. H. Lawrence's novel, in fact, portrayed the life of an immoral woman. The bishop replied: "It portrays the life of a woman in an immoral relationship, insofar as adultery is an immoral relationship."[5] The Archbishop of Canterbury (Dr. Geoffrey Fisher) was moved to indignant protest. "The Christian faith," he categorically affirmed, "is that adultery, whether in fact or in lustful longing, is always a sin. . . . The good pastor will teach his people to avoid both the fact of, and the desire for, sex experience of an adulterous kind and fornication also."[6] He rebuked the bishop for having appeared in the case, forthrightly adding, that he was "a stumbling block and a cause of offence to many ordinary Christians." It was shortly after these events that the bishop wrote his best seller, *Honest to God,* in which he vigorously affirmed that "the moral precepts of Jesus are not intended to be understood legalistically, as prescribing what all Christians must do, whatever the circumstances, and pronouncing certain courses of action universally right and others universally wrong."[7] What we need today, the bishop said, is "a radical 'ethic of the situation,' with nothing prescribed—except love."[8]

In a subsequent book, *Christian Morals Today,* the bishop wrote: "In Christian ethics the only pure statement is the command to love: every other injunction depends on it and is an explication or application of it."[9] "Love is the end, the *telos,* of the law not merely in the sense that it fulfils it (which it does), but in the sense that it abolishes it as the foundation of the Christian's

5 Rolph, *The Trial of Lady Chatterley,* p. 72.
6 *The Observer,* November 6, 1960.
7 (The Westminster Press, 1963), p. 110.
8 P. 116.
9 P. 16.

relationship whether with God or man."[10] The teaching of Jesus, he explained, was not the reform of legalism but its death.[11]

SITUATION ETHICS

Bishop Robinson acknowledges, in relation to the formulation of his views, his deep indebtedness to Joseph Fletcher, who, some years previously, had written an article for the *Harvard Divinity Bulletin*, entitled "The New Look in Christian Ethics." In the course of this article Fletcher advanced the view that what we need is a radical ethic of the situation. Concerning this thesis, Robinson said: "It is, of course, a highly dangerous ethic and the representatives of supernaturalistic legalism will, like the Pharisees, always fear it. Yet I believe it is the only ethic for 'man come of age.' "[12]

Fletcher subsequently wrote a book, *Situation Ethics: The New Morality*,[13] in which he expounds, in somewhat fuller detail, his interpretation of Christian ethics. As a caption, he cites the words of Tillich: "The law of love is the ultimate law because it is the negation of law; it is absolute because it concerns everything concrete. . . . The absolutism of love is its power to go into the concrete situation, to discover what is demanded by the predicament of the concrete to which it turns."[14]

In relation to the decision-making protest, Fletcher finds three alternative routes or approaches: (1) the legalistic; (2) the antinomian; (3) the situational. Concerning legalism, he observes: "Legalism in the Christian tradition has taken two forms. In the Catholic line it has been a matter of legalistic *reason,* based on nature or

10 P. 22.
11 P. 23.
12 *Honest to God*, p. 117.
13 (The Westminster Press, 1966.)
14 Quoted by Joseph Fletcher in *Situation Ethics*, p. 8.

natural law. These moralists have tended to adumbrate their ethical rules by applying human reason to the facts of nature, both human and subhuman, and to the lessons of historical experience. By this procedure they claim to have adduced universally agreed and therefore valid 'natural' moral laws. Protestant moralists have followed the same adductive and deductive tactics. They have taken Scripture and done with it what the Catholics do with nature. Their Scriptural moral law is, they argue, based on the words and sayings of the Law and the Prophets, the evangelists and apostles of the Bible. It is a matter of legalistic *revelation*. One is rationalistic, the other Biblicistic; one natural, the other Scriptural. But both are legalistic."[15]

"Over against legalism, as a sort of polar opposite," Fletcher posits antinomianism. "This is the approach with which one enters into the decision-making situation armed with no principles or maxims whatsoever, to say nothing of *rules*. In every 'existential moment' or 'unique' situation, it declares, one must rely upon the situation of itself, *there and then,* to provide its ethical solution."[16]

There is, Fletcher suggests, a third approach based upon an awareness that "circumstances alter cases."[17] "The situationist," he explains, "follows a moral law or violates it according to love's need."[18] "It is," he points out, "empirical, fact-minded, data conscious, inquiring. . . . It is sensitive to variety and complexity."[19] Again: "*Christian* situation ethics has only one norm or principle or law (call it what you will) that is binding and unexceptionable, always good and right regardless of the

15 *Op. cit.,* p. 21.
16 *Ibid.,* p. 22.
17 *Ibid.,* p. 29.
18 *Ibid.,* p. 26.
19 *Ibid.,* p. 29.

circumstances. That is 'love'—the *agape* of the summary commandment to love God and the neighbor. Everything else without exception, all laws and rules and principles and ideals and norms, are only *contingent,* only valid *if they happen* to serve love in any situation. Christian situation ethics is not a system or program of living according to a code, but an effort to relate love to a world of relativities through a casuistry obedient to love. It is the strategy of love."[20]

In a chapter on "Some Presuppositions," Fletcher stresses that situation ethics is pragmatic, relativistic, positivistic, and personalistic. Situation ethics, he agrees, involves a radical reversal of the classic approach. "It focuses on cases and tries experientially, not propositionally, to adduce, not deduce, some 'general' ideas to be held only tentatively and lightly. It deals with cases in all their contextual particularity, deferring in fear and trembling only to the rule of love. Situation ethics keeps principles sternly in their place, in the role of advisers without veto power!"[21]

Fletcher admits that there are those who say that situationism ignores the reality of human sin or egocentricity, and fails to appreciate the finitude of human reason, but this is only true, he suggests, of those who think there was literally once a fall and who think with Paul that we need a law to control us.[22]

LAW AND LOVE

But this is altogether too cavalier a verdict. Evangelicals agree that "love is the fulfilling of the law" (Rom. 13:10); what they deny is that "to fulfill" is the same as "to abrogate."

[20] *Ibid.,* p. 30.
[21] *Ibid.,* p. 55.
[22] *Ibid.,* p. 81.

The Reformers argued that the law serves three purposes. There is, in the first place, the civil use of law (*usus politicus*), to restrain evil men (I Tim. 1:8 f.); secondly, there is the use of law as a "schoolmaster" (*usus pedagogus*), to convict us of sin and to lead us to Christ (Gal. 3:24); thirdly, there is the use of law as a guide to the Christian life (*usus normativus*). In the words of the Formula of Concord (1577): "It is established that the Law of God was given to men for three causes: first, that a certain external discipline might be preserved, and wild and intractable men might be restrained, as it were, by certain barriers; secondly, that by the Law men might be brought to an acknowledgment of their sins; thirdly, that regenerate men, to all of whom, nevertheless, much of the flesh still cleaves, for that very reason may have some certain rule after which they may and ought to shape their life."

In the first place the law is a means of preservation. It sets a bound to the lawlessness of sinful men. It does this by providing rewards and punishments and the sanctions of force. It is the office of the law, Calvin writes, "by means of its fearful denunciations and consequent dread of punishment, to curb those who, unless forced, have no regard for rectitude or justice. . . . This forced and extorted righteousness is necessary for the good of society, its peace being secured by a provision but for which all things would be thrown into tumult and confusion."[23] He quotes, in this connection, the words of the apostle Paul: "But we know that the law is good, if a man use it lawfully; knowing this, that the law is not made for a righteous man, but for the lawless and disobedient, for the ungodly and for sinners, for unholy and profane, for murderers of fathers and murderers of mothers, for manslayers, for whoremongers, for them

23 *Institutes,* II. vii. 10.

that defile themselves with mankind, for menstealers, for liars, for perjured persons, and if there be any other thing that is contrary to sound doctrine; according to the glorious gospel of the blessed God, which was committed to my trust." (I Tim. 1:8–11.) It is God's will to preserve the world until the end of time, so that he who enforces law is in a very real sense "the minister of God" (Rom. 13:4). "The sanction that the Bible, here and elsewhere, gives to the forcible restraint of evil puzzles many Christians," writes A. R. Vidler. "But this comes from failing to distinguish the preservation from the salvation of the world. The truth is that the Bible affirms both the law 'which worketh wrath' (Rom. 4:15) and the 'faith which worketh by love' (Gal. 5:6): both Christ's strange work and His proper work." "We must behold," he says, "the severity as well as the goodness of God."[24]

"Both mercy and wrath," Vidler explains, "are expressions of God's fatherly care for mankind and of His gracious will to save the world, since, if it is to be saved, it must be preserved. God preserves the world by His wrath and justice in order that He may save it by His mercy and love."[25]

Secondly, the law is a summons to repentance. It convicts us of sin. "I had not known sin," Paul confesses, "but by the law." (Rom. 7:7.) "The law did not cause sin," Clement of Alexandria explains, "but showed sin."[26] The function of the law, Vidler states, "is to fix upon us the bondage of a salutary despair."[27] "The point of the law," Archbishop Leighton says, "pricks the heart, which is swelled, and puffed up with pride, and makes it fall

24 *Christ's Strange Work* (London: Longmans, Green & Co., Ltd., 1944), p. 28.
25 *Ibid.*, p. 30.
26 *Miscellanies,* ii. 7.
27 *Op. cit.*, p. 42.

low in a sense of vileness."[28] The law, by exposing our bankruptcy, drives us to the Savior.

Thirdly, the law provides guidance for the church. To deny that there is any place for law in the life of the church is the heresy of antinomianism. Calvin defines the third use of the law in these terms: "The third use of the Law (being also the principal use, and more closely connected with its proper end) has respect to believers in whose hearts the Spirit of God already flourishes and reigns. For although the Law is written and engraven on their hearts by the finger of God, that is, although they are so influenced and actuated by the Spirit that they desire to obey God, there are two ways in which they still profit in the Law. For it is the best instrument for enabling them daily to learn with greater truth and certainty what the will of the Lord is which they aspire to follow, and to confirm them in this knowledge. . . . Then, because we need not doctrine merely, but exhortation also, the servant of God will derive this further advantage from the Law: by frequently meditating upon it, he will be excited to obedience, and confirmed in it, and so drawn away from the slippery slopes of sin."[29] Christians, Vidler rightly observes, "are no longer under the bondage of the law, but it is still binding on them." "The preaching of the Gospel," he notes, "ought always to be followed as well as preceded by the teaching of the law." "God's law," he explains, "shows the regenerates the path that they should walk in, and warns them whenever they are straying from it."[30] That is why the godly man delights in the law of the Lord, and meditates in it day and night (Ps. 1:2). "Thy word," the psalmist joyfully exclaims, "is

28 Quoted in Vidler, *op. cit.*, p. 45.
29 *Institutes*, II. vii. 12.
30 *Op. cit.*, pp. 50, 52.

a lamp unto my feet, and a light unto my path." (Ps. 119:105.) "The Mosaic Law," Clement of Alexandria boldly affirms, "is the fountain of all ethics."[31]

It is their recognition of the reality of human sin or egocentricity, and the finitude of human reason, that causes evangelicals to stress that there is a place for the law in the life of the regenerate man. "Thus, although the Christians are liberated from the fear and bondage of the Law, from the impossible task of saving themselves by doing the works of the Law or by living up to the Sermon on the Mount, yet also they know that God's Law and commandments are still in force. The Law has still to be learned, and the duty of obedience to it has still to be proclaimed. For the Christians, however, the service of God no longer means 'doing the works of the Law,' but 'bringing forth the fruits of the Spirit.' "[32]

"Modern Christians," Fletcher states, in dogmatic fashion, "ought not to be naïve enough to accept any other view of Jesus' ethic than the situational one." And then, by way of emphatic example, he states: "Whether any form of sex (hetero, homo, or auto) is good or evil depends on whether love is fully served."[33] In a character-istic passage he writes: "The Christian ethic is not inter-ested in reluctant virgins and technical chastity. What sex probably needs more than anything is a good airing, demythologizing it and getting rid of its mystique-laden and occult accretions, which come from romanticism on the one hand and puritanism on the other. People are learning that we can have sex without love, and love without sex; that baby-making can be (and often ought to be) separated from love-making. It is, indeed, for rec-reation as well as for procreation. But if people do not

31 *Miscellanies,* ii. 18.
32 Vidler, *op. cit.,* p. 18.
33 *Op. cit.,* p. 139.

believe it is wrong to have sex relations outside marriage, it isn't, unless they hurt themselves, their partners, or others. This is, of course, a very big 'unless' and gives reason to many to abstain altogether except within the full mutual commitment of marriage. The civil law-makers are rapidly ridding their books of statutes making unmarried sex a crime between consenting adults. All situationists would agree with Mrs. Patrick Campbell's remark that they can do what they want 'as long as they don't do it in the street and frighten the horses.' "[34]

In answer to the question: Is adultery wrong? Fletcher offensively replies: "To ask this is to ask a mare's-nest question. It is a glittering generality, like Oscar Wilde's mackerel in the moonlight: it glitters but it stinks."[35] Ignoring the crudity of the remark we may well ask whether any stigma is good enough to beat a dogma.

In a review of *Situation Ethics* in *The Christian Century*,[36] James Gustafson observes that " 'love,' like 'situation,' is a word that runs through Fletcher's book like a greased pig." Fletcher, he complains, does not define his terms, neither is he consistent in his use of words. His thinking, Gustafson accuses, is "sloppy."

Paul Ramsey, in an important study, entitled *Deeds and Rules in Christian Ethics*,[37] subjects Fletcher's philosophy to further critical examination. "No social morality," Ramsey opines, "was founded, or ever will be founded, upon a situational ethic."[38] The Biblical covenant view of marriage, he points out, "affirms the will's competence to bind itself from one moment to another throughout all change"[39]: it presupposes and necessitates

34 *Ibid.*, p. 140.
35 *Ibid.*, p. 142.
36 May 18, 1966.
37 (Charles Scribner's Sons, 1967.)
38 P. 14.
39 P. 37.

the concept of steadfast love. "Marriage, traditionally and rightly understood, is something to which two people belong, in which they belong to one another and which belongs to neither of the parties. It is a rule of life and a moral bond. It is a cause between them and greater than they are or than any of the acts of love in marriage."[40] If God's love in binding himself to the world is the model for all our human covenants, then, it is clear, human love will also imply obligations that are unconditional and indissoluble.

Love, by its very nature, is exclusive: it is never promiscuous. (The expression "free love" is, of course, a contradiction in terms: if it is free, it is not love; if it is love, it is not free.)

Why should a couple who truly love one another (though unmarried) not express their love by means of physical intercourse? The answer is that, for most men, the acceptance of the privileges of marriage are conditional upon the prior acceptance of marriage's responsibilities.

Most couples, who desire to enjoy the blessing of Almighty God, will feel that it is fitting that they should publicly declare their intention of living together, by seeking, in the company of their friends, God's blessing upon their union as man and wife.

As members of a community, we are all wrapped together in the "bundle of life" (I Sam. 25:29). No man, Paul rightly insists, lives unto himself (Rom. 14:7). We owe a debt to the society of which we are members. As Christians, we are to do that which "is honorable not only in the Lord's sight but also in the sight of men" (II Cor. 8:21, RSV).

For Christians, the gift of chastity belongs to the altar of love, on which altar no gift is worthy that is not the

40 P. 38.

product of a pure intention and fruit of an entire dedication.

"The new morality," Prof. Henry Chadwick asserts, "takes the doctrine of the isolated individual to the point of hysteria."[41] True wisdom lies not in repudiating the past but in building on it. William Lillie pertinently points out that "the Bible makes a connection almost amounting to identification between loving God and keeping His commandments."[42] "The twentieth-century questioning of the categorical nature of the commands contained in the Sermon on the Mount and in the latter parts of St. Paul's Epistles," he warns, "may be due to the continued presence of an evil imagination in the heart of man (Genesis 6:5) and not to his having suddenly come of age." Commenting on Canon Montefiore's remark that "unless revealed law can be shown to be reasonable it lacks full authority and can only be obeyed by the sacrifice of the intellect,"[43] Lillie says: "Is not this one step towards the view that human reason is the sole arbiter of right and wrong—a view very flattering to human pride, but contrary both to the biblical witness as to the deceitfulness of the heart of man (Jeremiah 17:9), and to what modern psychology has shown of our proneness to rationalization?" That is why Christians ought to beware of separating God's guidance in the present from the lessons of the past. (It is fools, we are told, who find it necessary to learn by experience.) The things that happened long ago, Paul says, happened by way of example and "were written for our admonition, upon whom the ends of the

41 Report on the last of the Gifford Lectures at St. Andrew's University, *The Times*, April 30, 1964.

42 "Law and Love," *The Scottish Journal of Theology*, June, 1965.

43 *God, Sex and War*, by D. M. MacKinnon *et al.* (The Westminster Press, 1965), p. 78.

world are come" (I Cor. 10:11). It is through obedience to the Word of God, and humble submission to it, that we learn the mind of God. "He who looks into the perfect law," James writes, "the law of liberty, and perseveres, being no hearer that forgets but a doer that acts, he shall be blessed in his doing." (James 1:25, RSV.) And by the perfect law, the law of liberty, James means the written Word of God, that word which according to the writer of the epistle to the Hebrews, "is living and active, sharper than any two-edged sword, piercing to the division of soul and spirit, of joints and marrow, and discerning the thoughts and intentions of the heart" (Heb. 4:12, RSV).

Our recognition that God has spoken in the past does not preclude a recognition that God also speaks to us in the present. God, in the memorable words of John Owen, has yet much light to break forth from his Word. What we are promised, through the Spirit of God, is a growing understanding of truth and a deeper apprehension of it (John 16:13). The condition of blessing, as always, is obedience to the truth which we know. "The meek will he guide in judgment: and the meek will he teach his way." (Ps. 25:9.)

CHAPTER NINE

CONCLUSION

IN THE *Journal of His Life and Doings Amongst the North American Indians,* David Brainerd writes: "I never got away from Jesus, and Him Crucified, and I found that when my people were gripped by this great evangelical doctrine of Christ, and Him Crucified, I had no need to give them instructions about morality. I found that one followed as the sure and inevitable fruit of the other." Again: "I find my Indians begin to put on the garments of holiness, and their common life begins to be sanctified even in a trifle when they are possessed by the doctrine of Christ, and Him Crucified."[1]

There is, David Brainerd insists, a necessary and inescapable connection between faith and conduct, belief and practice.

Today, we are paying a heavy price for the repudiation of revealed religion. "Impoverish your creed," J. H. Jowett bluntly says, "and you sterilize your morality." "A devitalized theology," he insists, "creates a disabled and dispirited morality." "You cannot," he repeats, "expunge the theology and retain the morality."[2]

What is required, in the final analysis, for the rehabilitation of true morality and sanity in sex is a re-

---

[1] Quoted by J. H. Jowett in *Apostolic Optimism* (London: Hodder & Stoughton, Ltd., 1902), p. 84.
[2] *Op. cit.,* pp. 248, 254.

discovery of faith. It is an incontrovertible fact that, associated with the Reformation, there was a quickening of conscience and a heightened sense of sin. Protestantism gave birth to Puritanism and a revitalized theology found expression in a renewed and empowered morality. "I will show you," Wesley cried, "him that was a lion until then, and is now a lamb; him that was a drunkard, and is now exemplarily sober; the whoremonger that was, who abhors the very 'garment spotted by the flesh.' "[3]

Dorothy Sayers observes: "We have been trying for several centuries to uphold a particular standard of ethical values which derives from Christian dogma, while gradually dispensing with the very dogma which is the sole rational foundation for those values."[4] "It is worse than useless," she repeats, "for Christians to talk about the importance of Christian morality, unless they are prepared to take their stand upon the fundamentals of Christian theology."[5]

Professor F. J. Foakes-Jackson, in a neglected article in *Cambridge Theological Essays,* attributes the achievements of a former generation of evangelicals, in the field of humanitarian reform, to their Biblical theology. "Prison reform, the prohibition of the slave trade, the abolition of slavery, the Factory Acts, the protection of children, the crusade against cruelty to animals, all these things" were a product of "that form of Protestantism which is distinguished by the importance it attaches to the doctrine of the Atonement." "History shows," he continues, "that the thought of Christ on the Cross has been more potent than anything else in arousing a compassion for suffering and indignation at injustice." "Evangelical-

[3] Quoted by V. H. H. Green in *John Wesley* (Thomas Nelson & Sons, 1964), p. 75.
[4] *Creed or Chaos?* (London: Hodder & Stoughton, Ltd., 1940), p. 8.
[5] *Ibid.,* p. 12.

ism, which saw in the death of Christ the means of free salvation for fallen humanity, caused its adherents to take the front rank as champions of the weak, the feeling roused by their form of belief in the Atonement being summed up in the lines

> *"All this I did for thee:*
> *What hast thou done for me?"*[6]

Foakes-Jackson freely acknowledges that what moved these men on behalf of suffering humanity was their experience of Christ and him crucified.

It was a like evangelical experience that enabled men, in the early days of the church's story, to triumph over the degrading licentiousness of the Greco-Roman world. It was the Christian church, W. E. H. Lecky notes, in his *History of European Morals,* which established the principles on which Western civilization was founded, especially the principles of the sanctity of life, human brotherhood, the improved status of women, and sexual morality. "There is probably no other branch of ethics," he concedes, "which has been so largely determined by special dogmatic theology."[7]

Our most urgent need, for the reestablishment of pure morality, is the powerful preaching of Christ and him crucified. "Do men gather grapes of thorns, or figs of

6 (The Macmillan Company, 1905), pp. 512 f.
7 Cf. "It was reserved for Christianity to present to the world an ideal character, which through all the changes of eighteen centuries has inspired the hearts of men with an impassioned love; has shown itself capable of acting on all ages, nations, temperaments and conditions; has been not only the highest pattern of virtue but the strongest incentive to its practice; and has exercised so deep an influence that it may be truly said that the simple record of three short years of active life has done more to regenerate and to soften mankind than all the disquisitions of philosophers, and all the exhortations of moralists" (London: Longmans, Green & Co., Ltd., 1911), Vol. ii, p. 8. Cf. Vol. ii, p. 100.

thistles?" Jesus asked. (Matt. 7:16.) "If the root be holy," Paul explained, "so are the branches." (Rom. 11:16.) Without the root of faith we cannot expect the fruit of holiness. That is why our most urgent task, in this age, as in every age, is the fearless and faithful preaching of Christ and him crucified.